YOU'RE N
IF

FREE AT WORK,
WHERE ARE YOU
FREE?

LITERATURE AND SOCIAL CHANGE
SELECTED ESSAYS AND INTERVIEWS 1994-2014

ESSENTIAL ESSAYS SERIES 69

ONTARIO ARTS COUNCIL
CONSEIL DES ARTS DE L'ONTARIO
an Ontario government agency
un organisme du gouvernement de l'Ontario

Canada Council   Conseil des arts
for the Arts   du Canada

Guernica Editions Inc. acknowledges the support of the Canada
Council for the Arts and the Ontario Arts Council. The Ontario Arts
Council is an agency of the Government of Ontario.
We acknowledge the financial support of the Government of Canada.

Tom Wayman

IF YOU'RE NOT
FREE AT WORK,
WHERE ARE YOU
FREE?

LITERATURE AND SOCIAL CHANGE
SELECTED ESSAYS AND INTERVIEWS 1994-2014

GUERNICA
EDITIONS

TORONTO · BUFFALO · LANCASTER (U.K.)
2018

Michael Mirolla, editor
Guernica Editions Inc.
Cover Design: David Moratto
Interior Design: Rafael Chimicatti
1569 Heritage Way, Oakville, (ON), Canada L6M 2Z7
2250 Military Road, Tonawanda, N.Y. 14150-6000 U.S.A.

Distributors:
University of Toronto Press Distribution,
5201 Dufferin Street, Toronto (ON), Canada M3H 5T8
Gazelle Book Services, White Cross Mills
High Town, Lancaster LA1 4XS U.K.

First edition.
Printed in Canada.

Legal Deposit – First Quarter
Library of Congress Catalogue Card Number: 2017960391
Library and Archives Canada Cataloguing in Publication

Wayman, Tom, 1945-
[Essays. Selections]
If you're not free at work, where are you free? : literature
and social change : selected essays and interviews 1994-2014 / Tom
Wayman.

Issued in print and electronic formats.
ISBN 978-1-77183-287-8 (softcover).--ISBN 978-1-77183-288-5
(EPUB).--ISBN 978-1-77183-289-2 (Kindle)

1. Literature and society. 2. Essays. I. Title.

PS8595.A9A6 2018   C814'.54   C2017-907293-5
                                    C2017-907294-3

OTHER BOOKS BY TOM WAYMAN

COLLECTIONS OF POEMS:
Waiting For Wayman (1973)
For And Against The Moon (1974)
Money And Rain (1975)
Free Time (1977)
A Planet Mostly Sea (1979)
Living On The Ground (1980)
Introducing Tom Wayman: Selected Poems 1973-80 (1980)
The Nobel Prize Acceptance Speech (1981)
Counting The Hours (1983)
The Face of Jack Munro (1986)
In a Small House on the Outskirts of Heaven (1989)
Did I Miss Anything? Selected Poems 1973-1993 (1993)
The Astonishing Weight of the Dead (1994)
I'll Be Right Back: New & Selected Poems 1980-1996 (1997)
The Colours of the Forest (1999)
My Father's Cup (2002)
High Speed Through Shoaling Water (2007)
Dirty Snow (2012)
Winter's Skin (2013)
The Order in Which We Do Things: The Poetry of Tom Wayman
(ed. Owen Percy; 2014)
Built to Take It: Selected Poems 1996-2013 (2014)
Helpless Angels (2017)

FICTION:
Boundary Country (2007)
A Vain Thing (2007)
Woodstock Rising (2009)
The Shadows We Mistake for Love (2015)

NON-FICTION:
Inside Job: Essays on the New Work Writing (1983)
A Country Not Considered: Canada, Culture, Work (1993)
Songs Without Price: The Music of Poetry in a Discordant World (2008)

EDITED:
Beaton Abbot's Got The Contract (1974)
A Government Job At Last (1976)
Going For Coffee (1981; 1987)
East of Main (co-edited with Calvin Wharton; 1989)
Paperwork (1991)
The Dominion of Love (2001)

We like the word "abstract." Sometime we like the word "language" too much. But if we use those words in a community, we wouldn't get anywhere. So maybe the word "role" is better. So one of the roles is community. If you can get your poem into a community ... then you will have opened up a large, beautiful gate that is going to lead you to beauty, wisdom, and community, and warmth, and heart, as opposed to paper, text, pat on the back, and black coffee.

—Juan Filipe Herrera, California Poet Laureate 2012-2014; U.S. Poet Laureate 2015-2017

TABLE OF CONTENTS

If You're Not Free At Work, Where Are You Free?

Voices murmur concerning a "work/life balance"
or reverberate with conviction about
"our revered parliamentary heritage"
or intone why municipal tax subsidies are needed
to persuade someone to finance
a new mall. The words surge and drop and swell
like the fluctuating clamour of the drunken dinner parties
—symposiums—where the ebb and flow of wit
created the concept of democracy,
while around the guests
the lash, shackles, branding iron
ensured that grains and animals were raised
and brought to market, the meal was concocted
and served; locked windows and beatings
that resulted in broken limbs and teeth, permanent hearing loss
meant grapes were harvested, wine fermented,
bedchambers readied. Days, years of hopeless sweat,
the shattering of families
caused fresh flowers to be grown, cut,
arranged amid the company in vases
other slaves threw on wheels slick with wet mud
—flowers also placed
along the Senate's benches
in preparation for the next debate.

INTRODUCTION

The Art of Work

This book, a selection of my essays and interviews from the past twenty years, for the most part continues the exploration of an absence, some of whose aspects and implications were discussed in my previous essay collections, *Inside Job: Essays on the New Work Writing* (1983) and *A Country Not Considered: Canada, Culture, Work* (1993). The absence that is my ongoing concern is a missing accurate depiction in art of the effects of people's daily employment on their lives on and off the job. For instance, in the literary world anyone can attend a writers' festival, or scan the shelves of a bookstore, or prowl the aisles of publishers' displays at a book fair and never hear or see any indication that the central and governing experience of people's daily existence, and the place where the community's goods and services—along with their attendant social hierarchies of wealth and power—are created, is the workplace. Most literary anthologies offer a portrait of a nation in which nobody works. Visit a series of art galleries, take in a ballet or other dance performance, and the result is the same.

The rare exceptions to this situation only serve to underline the pervasiveness of the absence. This vacancy occurs despite a continual assurance by proponents of the arts that the latter have value because they tell humanity's story, and in so doing provide vital insights that enhance our existence. "[Artists'] work inspires the reflection so needed to make sense of the complexity of our lives," Robert Sirman, director and CEO of the Canada Council for the Arts from 2006 to 2014, writes in the *Literary Review of Canada* (22.8 October 2014). "Artists may not be the creators of the city or the faith or the imagination, but they are critical to their animation and vitality, and through their reflective capacity help each of us better understand who we are and what it means to be human."

The hollowness of this claim, in the face of the absence of a consideration of the tremendous impact of our jobs on our own and our neighbours' lives, on our humanity, echoes the hollowness of earlier generations' pronouncements about "Man's" achievements in literature or other artistic endeavours during a period when accurate representations of women's experiences were invisible. As now, the few exceptions back then to the deficiency not only underscored how widespread the absence was, but also pointed the way forward to a time when literature and the other arts would be transformed by the presence of what had formerly been ignored or concealed.

The still-pending transformation of the arts I mention in my writing will involve *both* genders, since the work of all of us—blue- and white-collar, paid and unpaid labour—reproduces society each day. Yet, as I discuss in the essays reprinted here, just as the incorporation into art of an accurate depiction of women's lives required the emergence of an effective social movement committed to realizing women's equality, so the pending artistic transformation will not occur without the emergence of forces dedicated to the implementation of democracy in the workplace.

The latter is not a new idea. Just as the concepts of women's worth, rights, and liberation flared and dimmed for centuries before its current successes and energetic ongoing struggles, so workplace emancipation has been a goal ever since one man employed another. Most recently, the idea of employees' rights is not only the philosophical foundation of unionism, but three times in the twentieth century societies emerged that sought to institutionalize citizens' democratic control of their working lives, and by extension the economy. That these attempts to bring democracy to the workplace all were crushed by the armed forces of reaction no more invalidates humanity's longing for this goal than the setbacks the women's movement has experienced, and still faces, invalidate the reality of women as fully functional persons, entitled to the same freedoms and opportunities available to men.

Indeed, an example of the persistence of the idea of jobsite democracy can be found in the same issue of the *Literary Review of Canada* in which the outgoing head of the Canada Council repeats the standard bromides about the value of contemporary art. In reviewing Tom Malleson's *After Occupy: Economic Democracy for the 21st Century*, Peter MacLeod notes that "outside of formal politics, democratic societies practice very little of what might properly be called democracy. Economic systems are rarely empathetic or participatory and as the debacles of the past decade have once again shown, markets are far from responsible."

MacLeod is the co-founder of MASS LBP, a Toronto public consultation firm whose spinoff, the Wagemark Foundation, offers certification to companies and non-profits who keep the gap between their CEO and the lowest-paid employee to below 8:1. In contrast, in 2010 the ratio of remuneration between the 100 highest paid CEOs of Canadian companies on the Toronto Stock Exchange and the average Canadian wage was 189:1 (a ratio that represents a raise of 27 per cent for executives over the previous year).

In his review, MacLeod states some of the points my essays below make: "If achieving responsible government was the democratic project of the 19th and 20th centuries, achieving responsible economics and a universal economic franchise is a fitting objective for the 21st." MacLeod emphasizes, as I do, the need, in envisioning and ultimately implementing this project, of multiple approaches to solving the problems economic emancipation involves: "[T]he cause of economic democracy needs the biggest possible tent." And MacLeod identifies the conundrum of how to ensure an innovative spirit in a collective enterprise. Where he and I part company is at his belief that the answer lies in "making real a more modern, democratic form of capitalism."

Whatever shapes economic liberation takes, though, the literature that accompanies it, or that accompanies the organizations struggling to achieve it, will include the traditional literary subjects of love, death and nature—however a foregrounding of employment's influence on our responses to these topics affects how they are depicted. And since we live our lives at the local level—despite the current frantic efforts of the corporations to insist we live in cyberspace, or in some consumerist or celebrity fantasyland—the new literature will involve an exploration of the pleasures and challenges of the local (home, neighbourhood, family, biosphere, ancestry, language). Portraying how the work we do impacts, and is impacted by, these facets of the local, will keep fingers flying over keyboards for a long, long time. Yet only when our working lives are widely understood to be important enough to warrant occurring in a democratic environment will art that engages the myriad dimensions and implications of our employment experiences be valued as depicting the core of the human story.

Looking toward that better future, I've included in the present collection, besides ruminations on literature and work, pieces on love, and on the combative resilience of one geographic locale with which I've been involved for decades. Since art, and the teaching of art, like any trades have a history and a present configuration arising from that history, I offer here also essays on poetry, the teaching of poetry, and a post-Sixties development in the arts and social sciences intended to ensure the latter human endeavours do not contribute to beneficial social change. All these topics are further explored in four interviews, where I feel the excellent questions offered by the interviewers provided an opportunity to further consider the issues these themes involve.

While I believe the literature of the future that the present book predicts is inevitable, I have to acknowledge that the second decade of the twenty-first century appears a particularly bleak time to invoke a development in society, and hence in the arts, that depends on a major rethinking of what constitutes a self-governing community or nation, and on the appearance or revitalization of organizations committed to the struggle to realize the extension of democracy to the workplace. After all, the Occupy movement, which wrestled with a number of the issues considered in the present book and which is one of the few North American manifestations this century of a popular will to implement beneficial social change, did not originate with any of our contemporary institutions that are supposedly advocates for and/or facilitators of a better life: unions, churches, and postsecondary campuses.

So far the twenty-first century has little to recommend it, offering the same characteristics as marked the start of the twentieth century: permanent war overseas, uncontested seizure of increasing amounts of society's wealth by a handful of bosses, religious extremism, and the reduction of Canada's economy to a source of raw materials for the dominant world economic powers. Our present society, distracted by electronic devices falsely promising greater communication and thus greater community, and by a pervasive celebrity culture, may have replaced a society blinkered by blind loyalty to the colonial homeland masquerading as patriotism. But the threat of climate change and its social and economic consequences perhaps casts a shadow forward even darker than how the slaughterhouses of two world wars, the decade of the Great Depression, and life under the omnipresent threat of nuclear annihilation loomed ahead, as we now know, at the start of the twentieth century.

My optimism regarding the liberation of work originates in my belief that a widespread reconsideration of what a self-governing society might look like, a reconsideration such as we saw in the 1930s and the 1960s in North America, will come again, albeit involving attitudes and social action as different from and similar to those occurring in these tumultuous periods as attitudes and events in these periods were different from and similar to each other. I take comfort and hope, too, in how humanity as a species has triumphed over one world-shaking crisis after another, and also in how, if seen from a long enough perspective, humanity's march has ever been toward a freer, happier life for an increasing number of our planet's inhabitants despite all the roadblocks encountered and retreats endured. Though many members of our species remain in physical and/or mental bondage, the slow tide of history has buoyed an always-increasing number toward a life free of subjection to kings, priests, and arbitrary authority of every sort.

And no prevailing ideology or off-the-job distractions can entirely disguise work, as presently organized, as being a place of servitude for so many. The obviousness of the situation is evident, for instance, upon a few moments' reflection on the catchphrases "freedom 55" or "work-life balance." Nor do an individual's dreams of, or even attainment of, escape from externally imposed employment hierarchies permit that individual to escape from existence in a society where the rest of the inhabitants and institutions are malformed by the conditions under which daily work is currently organized. Since the flood of history flows from unelected authority toward social freedom, however, work cannot forever remain a locale not yet transformed by democracy. Nor can the ways human lives are centrally shaped by our employment forever exist as a peripheral or nonexistent concern of art.

That said, let me briefly stress that my essays and interviews collected here are not about class. One hangover of the 1930s is that when someone starts talking about work, some people assume the conversation is about the working *class*. As I observe in an essay not included in the present volume, "Work and Silence" (the afterword to a 2014 selected poems of mine edited by Owen Percy, *The Order in Which We Do Things*), a focus on class, rather than work "frequently shifts attention from the specifics of a jobsite to family stories—see, for instance, M.L. Liebler's anthology *Working Words* [2010]." In the academy, "gestures toward class often substitute, in my experience, for thinking about work: class is trotted out along with race and gender (and/or sex) as a nontraditional, supposedly fresh way to look at literature." Yet the critic Eric Schocket has argued, as I note, that "these alternative critical approaches are far from parallel." Schocket maintains, in Vanishing *Moments: Class and American Literature* (2006), that race, gender and sexuality "name social relationships that are not structured by an unequal distribution of power (this is the dream of pluralism, after all)." But class, Schocket insists, "can only name a structure, process or position of inequality." He quotes critic John Guillory as insisting that, given the origins of class stratification, while there is much admirable about working-class culture, to affirm an identity based on that culture is to base such an affirmation on injustice, unlike affirming a positive racial, gender or sexual identity. Moreover, Schocket demonstrates how a consideration of social mobility (an individual or family's escape from a particular kind of wage labour—often a topic when class is considered) hides, as I say in my essay, "the actual conditions of a job that others must endure once certain individuals or their descendants have found different employment."

Thus in the pertinent writing here I try to keep my attention on daily work and its specific social and personal effects, and on work's potential inclusion in art. Overall, in preparing the present volume, I have slightly revised in places some essays and interviews since their original publication in the interests of clarity, and especially to reduce or eliminate the repetition of certain ideas found in these pieces in their first published form. Where a concept *is* repeated in this book in a subsequent essay or interview, I have retained such repetition because the discussion in this case involves an aspect or amplification of the idea not present in its earlier appearance.

Some essays quote passages included in my earlier critical collections. The initial essay here, "To Be Free Full-Time," particularly does so in an attempt to bring a reader who has not read the earlier volumes up to date, as it were, on my thinking before the essay moves forward into new territory. In other pieces where I loop back to refer to matters I have considered in previously collected essays, my original goal was to recast my observations and conclusions into fresh language. At times, though, the rewrite never worked as well as my previous articulation of an idea, so I revert to offering my earlier wording.

One interview in this book, as noted in the Acknowledgements, was longer in manuscript than as originally published. Where I liked the questions asked that ultimately were not in the printed version (and where, obviously, I liked my answers to such questions), I have included them. Conversely, as noted, where published interviews repeat material already presented in essays or interviews that appear earlier in this book, I cut such matter, rendering the interview offered here shorter than the original published version.

"Appledore"
Winlaw, BC

WORKING CONDITIONS
Essays

TO BE FREE FULL-TIME
The Challenge of Work

An accurate examination of people's experiences in the workforce is, with few exceptions, missing from our contemporary cultural productions, our educational curriculums, our news and entertainment media, and advertising. I have written elsewhere of how this absence occurs despite how work, for a majority of us, is the central and governing experience of daily life. Work determines, for example, our standard of living, how much time and energy we have before and after going to our jobs, the place we live. Our employment has a major influence on who are friends are, and strongly affects our attitudes towards an enormous array of events, social movements, artifacts, environments, etc. And despite the silence in which our society wraps participation in the workforce, our jobs each day reconstruct society. Because of our efforts at work, the members of our community are fed, sheltered, clothed, educated, entertained, and much more.

The taboo surrounding a true insider's representation of everyday jobs is not a neutral fact, but a source of pain. As I argue in my 1993 collection of essays, *A Country Not Considered*:

[B]ecause work is not considered culturally important, school curriculums largely ignore the history, present form and possible future of daily employment. As a result, students frequently embark on years of training for a trade or profession with only the vaguest or glossiest notion of what a job is like and of how this employment affects the human beings who perform it. The absence in our culture of any accurate depiction of our work also leads to a profound sense of isolation. We are aware we have certain problems at the job, or problems that arise away from work because of our employment. But perhaps we are the only ones who feel this way? Left unsure and isolated, we are less likely to search for a collective answer to our difficulties, a collective means to improve our lives.

A further negative consequence of the taboo is a mystification of how products and services come to exist. One consequence of this mystification is that when we do not know much about each other's jobs, do not know much about how the goods and services we need or want are created, it becomes easier to believe negative reports about people who in reality are very much like ourselves. That is, we are willing to accept the received idea that postal workers are lazy, people on strike are greedy, etc. ("Laramie" 24)

Other ways the taboo is hurtful include ignorance on the part of employees of their legal rights concerning the workplace or work-related programs such as employment insurance, or how to redress injustices concerning the job or job-related issues. Not least as a source of harm is the diminishment of our sense of personal contribution to society, of the value and importance of what most of us do for a living.

Since our society has adopted such a pervasive aversion to a clear portrayal of our jobs and their consequences, there must be a *reason* why this taboo is in place. The considerable hurt that the maintenance of this taboo causes indicates that a powerful explanation must exist as to why such a fundamental human experience as everyday employment, one so basic to the existence of individuals and the community, can be so ignored. Part of understanding the taboo is surely to consider the cause or origin of it. What happens to us at work each day that makes us anxious to do nearly *anything* rather than examine this central dimension to our lives?

One frequent answer I hear is that work is a taboo subject because for much of the population work is boring. Gatekeepers of culture adopt this perspective, in my experience, in order to maintain that an accurate depiction of daily work is not a suitable topic for art. I find this response appears in some reviews of my collections of contemporary poems by Americans and Canadians about their jobs. In the introduction to *A Country Not Considered* I provide the following example:

> Why should we have to read, asked one newspaper reviewer of my most recent (1991) anthology, *Paperwork*, "about a reality from which we try, vicariously or otherwise, to escape?" The reviewer quoted William Faulkner as stating that since work is the only activity people do for eight hours a day, no wonder people are so miserable.
>
> Yet if the central experience of each day is so boring, and makes us so miserable, would it not follow that art would be the perfect place to assess what happens on the job? After all, the arts are usually touted as humanity's way of exploring existence, of expressing what it means to be human. In fact, the new writing about work in no way describes work as simply boring or miserable. Instead, it depicts the workplace as a locale where the entire range of human emotions are found—not excluding boredom and misery, but also including accomplishment, danger, joy, humour, rage, romanticism, whimsy, inquisitiveness, and much, much more. How could it be otherwise, since the jobsite is a place where human beings gather each day to live, interact, produce, in fact re-create the entire society? The new work writing shows that the range of personalities at work, and responses to the job, are as wide as humanity

itself. I am convinced that only somebody with a need to cling to a denial of what actually occurs on the job could attempt to reduce such a significant human experience to "boring" and "miserable." (8)

I have to add, too, that if work is so boring, why do people in conversation—even after a ritualistic disclaimer about the dullness of their jobs—talk about their work so animatedly once they know a listener is interested? Descriptions of personalities, events, tools, tasks, exceptional good days and bad days on the job and a great deal else pour out of people if the person to whom they are speaking displays any interest in breaking the silence that wraps the everyday workplace. Thus I conclude that the boringly repetitive part of the work process on many jobs cannot account for the existing taboo. Since work is so central to human life, I believe another factor besides the supposed one-dimensionality of employment experiences is the root of society's refusal to countenance a clear and honest examination of the job.

I believe the taboo against an accurate depiction of daily employment arises because we are not free at work. For most of us, democracy ceases the moment we cross the office door or the factory gate. Once we have clocked in, or otherwise have begun the working day, we are subject to authority which we have absolutely no voice in choosing. At our jobs, we are often ordered about like children. We usually have little or no control over the conditions of our employment, over the quality of the product or service our work creates, over the good or harm caused to other people by the product or service we make, and over how the wealth generated by our labour with muscle and brain will be used.

It is as though when we show up at work we cross through a time tunnel back to the era when the majority of people like ourselves did not have the vote in society and were expected to be dutifully obedient to their social "betters"—the representatives of various inherited authoritarian structures. The moment we appear at work, the democratic rights and privileges which as citizens we are assured continually by educators, politicians, and the media are the foundation of our society are all suspended. If in the midst of what we are told repeatedly is a political democracy we find such a lack of freedom at the heart of our day, at the heart of our lives, no wonder this glaring contradiction must be cloaked in silence and denial.

I describe the situation on the job as follows, in the introduction to my 1993 selected poems, *Did I Miss Anything?*:

> Briefly, we live our productive lives—the majority of our waking hours—as free-lance serfs. We are free to choose and change the masters we will obey for money, free to be destitute or marginal, free to go into debt, free to purchase as many of life's necessities and/or drugs and toys as our rate of remuneration permits. We are even free to employ other serfs. But most of us at work have no significant control over what happens to us, over who gives us orders, over the organization of production, over the distribution of the wealth our labour produces, over the social uses of what we create. The alternative of self-employment often turns into self-exploitation as we strive to remain competitive with enterprises employing serfs. (14)

Our working life means we endure what I call in one essay "this bizarre existence, where we are expected to alternate every few hours between being freedom-loving, responsible citizens of a democratic community while off the job, and docile, unquestioning respecters of authority while at work" ("Sitting" 177). I am convinced this schizoid existence accounts for many of our failures as effective members of the community—as parents, as citizens, as stewards of the planet. If we are treated as though we are half-witted or a child during the hours each day at our jobs, how can we suddenly transform ourselves into reasonable, rational adults the moment we climb into our car or board the bus after work? What attitudes toward ourselves do we take home from the job, after eight hours or more of being assured we lack the right or ability to make responsible decisions, to exercise control individually or with our peers over the manifold aspects of the work process?

Abraham Lincoln in June 1868 quoted St. Mark as maintaining that a house divided against itself cannot stand. Lincoln argued that, similarly, a government "cannot endure permanently half slave and half free" (Bartlett 537). Equally evident, I believe, is that the tensions caused in people by the endless shuttling between expectations of freedom and of serfdom, and between the behaviours demanded by such different social roles, are a contributing factor to a wide spectrum of personal dysfunction and collapse.

This unhealthy situation is compounded by the existing taboo. Therapists have tried to show how denial of a familial problem like alcoholism or child abuse vastly increases the damage such dysfunctions cause. Such a problem cannot be healed as long as no one will admit the dysfunction exists. In addition, young people especially are affected because the child learns that what she or he knows to be true is regarded by everyone around the child as false, and what the child knows is untrue is considered by everyone around the child as real. Everyone in the family, of every age, has to adopt elaborately irrational behaviours to establish and maintain the denial.

Similarly, when nothing in the surrounding culture admits to the lack of freedom at work experienced by an individual, the dysfunctional behaviour generated in the individual by experiencing such unfreedom is made worse by this blanket of denial. How can anyone discover and practice truthful and helpful social behaviour, when society is united in not admitting to the core condition that adversely affects so many of its members?

In the introduction to *A Country Not Considered* I give an example of how this denial worsens the personal and social ill caused by the lack of freedom at work. My intent is to consider the current behaviour of the citizens of the countries formerly under the sway of the U.S.S.R., and of the people of Quebec in my own country.

> On the planet at present, the inhabitants of many nations are demanding independence for their ethnic, religious or language group. And that is well and good. But after the shouting or the shooting stops, on the morning after the

victory celebrations whether deep in Eastern Europe or in Quebec, most people will file back through the office door or factory gate to a condition of servitude. The person who controls them there may now be of the same ethnic or religious or linguistic background as themselves. But the humiliation will continue. To me it is no wonder that the citizens of newly independent states often quickly feel cheated, wronged, short-changed, and turn on each other in civil wars or search out some scapegoat from among their fellow citizens on which to place the blame for the lack of freedom they still feel. This is the price of denial of the central fact of political and personal life. (7)

Because the absence of democracy at work is all we have known, the situation is conceived of by us as normal or organic, as though the state of unfreedom on the job is the result of some law of nature. But the hierarchical manner of organizing contemporary work is merely a continuation of the means by which jobs were structured during the Industrial Revolution in the second half of the eighteenth century—a time when the majority of people had absolutely no vote in the affairs of their community or nation. Nor is there any Holy Commandment that decrees: "The workplace shalt not be organized democratically." To date the human race has substantially done away with such long-entrenched practices as the divine right of kings, slavery, and the restriction of democracy to property owners or other possessors of wealth. All these ideas, like the subjugation of women, once were regarded as natural, approved by religious thought, and imposed by brute force.

When we see the workplace not as an unchanging, naturally occurring hierarchy, but instead regard the job as a social location not yet reached by the historical expansion of democracy, a vast range of possibilities for the organization of daily work can be considered. At present, if I have a job of work that I cannot do alone, I hire you. Both of us expect that because I give you money for your time and skills, you will unquestioningly obey my commands concerning the task I have assigned you. Yet a different way of regarding this scenario is that the moment I cannot complete a job alone, the moment I have to hire you to help me accomplish this work, then *two* people are engaged in completing the task. The money that I possess does not automatically endow me with dictatorial power over you. Instead, the two people who are working on this job decide together a wide range of matters connected with the work with which we are *both* involved. An analogy to this way of perceiving employment is that our society does not limit the exercise of the political franchise only to people who have acquired a certain level of personal wealth, skill, experience, or knowledge. In theory, every citizen has the vote regardless of his or her bank balance or what functions she or he performs (or doesn't perform) in the community.

Yet the taboo against a clear portrayal of employment perpetuates the idea that how we currently organize work is divinely or naturally ordained, and that no other possibilities are seriously open to consideration. As a result, we are prevented from beginning the protracted debate over a host of alternative arrangements, a debate that is absolutely essential if we are ever to democratize the hours we are employed. The belief that work naturally excludes democracy is as deeply and widely present in our society as the taboo. This belief in the organic nature of undemocratic jobs persists even though most of us have experienced non-hierarchically-organized work—a group of volunteers building an adventure playground on behalf of a community centre or church, or a group of friends constructing a dock at the summer cottage owned by one of them.

So established in our consciousness is the equation of employment with unfreedom that an awareness of the lack of democracy at work can change our political sense of the world. For me,

> I now see politics as authoritarian vs. anti-authoritarian, rather than in terms of left vs. right. And for me, the real test of the presence of democracy is what everyday work is like in a country, community or organization. I find this test more useful as a means of analysing what occurs in the world than some of my former ideas. Otherwise, how could I explain the odd coincidence that both a "right-wing"

> political group like B.C.'s Social Credit party [now call-
> ing itself the B.C. Liberal party] and a "left-wing" political
> group like, say, any former East European communist party,
> both propose the *identical* program for labour? Both, if you
> scrape the rhetoric off what they say, want all strikes banned
> on pain of jail or worse, and unions either powerless or at
> the very least regulated by the government in order to exist.
> No political party or government in the world wants
> democracy extended to the workplace. I have come to see
> this fact as basic to the politics of our era. ("Aspirin" 136-7)

Yet the critique of the lack of democracy on the job I have outlined here is hardly unique to our time. As long as there have been human beings, there have been voices that rejected the concept of the divine right of a privileged group to command others. The lack of freedom at work has been denounced almost from the inception of the hierarchical workplace. In North America during the nineteenth and twentieth centuries, we have seen within the trade union movement a tension between two very different conceptions of unions—one of which incorporates the ideas I am discussing here. In one vision, a union's role is to barter for the greatest possible return to serfs for their labour: best wages and benefits, most protection from arbitrary authority, and so on. In return, this form of union offers employers a policing of the workforce, an assurance to management of docile obedience overall to the job hierarchy established and maintained by the company and modified by contracts (collective agreements) between the employer and the union. This is business unionism, which in its present form is represented by the AFL-CIO, or in my country by the CLC, the Canadian Labour Congress. In general, business unionism is content with the taboo against an accurate portrayal of contemporary jobs, because discussion of more democratic methods of organizing work would force the union into a more antagonistic position with regard to unelected authority. Such a position would threaten the business union's ability to cut a deal with the boss, trading freedom for an orderly, regularly paid, somewhat-protected serfdom.

But alongside this vision of unionism is one held by men and women whose analysis of the workplace includes a rejection of the lack of democracy there. Since the start of the last century, the most dramatic embodiment of this form of unionism in North America is the Industrial Workers of the World, whose founding principles include not only employee takeover and management of industry, but also the abolition of wages in favour of democratic means of controlling and distributing the wealth produced by an enterprise. The I.W.W. flourished between 1905 and the 1920s, but was badly damaged by the attacks of government and employers against it in response to the labour turmoil during and after the First World War. The Russian Revolution of 1917 (whose implications for working people were not as evident immediately as they are now), the post-war employee unrest and civic general strikes such as that in Vancouver in 1918 and in Winnipeg and Seattle in 1919, all generated an intellectual and activist ferment among working men and women such that the ultimate victory of business unionism—and the preservation of undemocratic workplaces—was by no means assured. The I.W.W. took the fall for the set of ideas which seemed so threatening to the existing hierarchies, although these ideas (and even a tiny rump version of the I.W.W.) are found in the workforce today. But the taboo against an accurate depiction of daily work—a taboo which the I.W.W. sought valiantly to break through its songs, art, storytelling and literature—also has contributed to a reduction of the revolutionary form of unionism to a minuscule role at present. And the effect on working people of the effective disappearance of revolutionary unionism may be illustrated most by looking at changes in hours of work. Between 1900 and 1940, the four decades that encompass the heyday of an alternate vision for labour, average hours of employment per week dropped from eighty to forty. During the next forty years from 1940 to 1980, spanning the entrenching of business unionism, the work week remained constant at forty hours.

The ideas represented by the emergent I.W.W. appeared un-American to the power structure of its time. Yet the union itself did not think so. On June 27, 1905, in Brand's Hall in Chicago, Big Bill Haywood, General Secretary of the Western Federation of Miners, gavelled the meeting to order that would establish the I.W.W. out of an amalgam of existing unions, union locals, and individuals. Haywood's opening words were: "In calling this convention to order I do so with a sense of the responsibility that rests upon me and rests upon every delegate that is here assembled. This is the Continental Congress of the working class" (*Founding* 1).

The two hundred-odd delegates in Brand's Hall that June morning could make the connection between the goals of the founding fathers of American independence and their own intent in launching the new labour organization. Just as Congress was ultimately to reject the idea of British authority over the activities and resources of the colonists, so Haywood and the others opposed the undemocratic control of their working lives by the owners and managers of industry. As Haywood explained in a speech on the evening of July 7: "While we are going to do everything that we can to improve and take advantage of every opportunity that is offered to us to improve the condition of the working class as we go along, the ultimate aim of this organization is to get control of the supervision of industry" (*Founding* 579). In brief, the founders of the I.W.W. saw themselves as applying to the government of *enterprises* what Thomas Jefferson and the other members of the Continental Congress had concluded about the government of *nations*:

> We hold these truths to be self-evident; that all men are created equal; that they are endowed by their creator with certain unalienable rights; that among these are life, liberty and the pursuit of happiness; that to secure these rights, governments are instituted among men, deriving their just powers from the consent of the governed; that whenever any form of government becomes destructive to these ends, it is the right of the people to alter or to abolish it, and to institute new government, laying its foundation on such principles, and organizing its powers in such form, as to them shall seem most likely to effect their safety and happiness. (Bartlett 373)

The members of the first Congress were opposed to taxation without representation. Similarly, the delegates to the I.W.W.'s founding convention believed the introduction of democracy to the workplace would end the exclusion of themselves from the decisions that divide up the wealth produced by the labour of all employees. These decisions determine how much of the enterprise's income goes for purchase of raw materials, how much is earmarked for research and development, how much is put aside for contingencies and for the eventual replacement of physical plant, how much is returned to investors, and how much is allotted to the men and women who perform the work that results in the enterprise's income—including agreeing on the disparity in remuneration, if one is to exist, between managerial and productive tasks. The present monopoly by management of the decision-making concerning this wealth means money is taken from employees and put to various uses by management without the employees' consent. If in 1776 Britain's "right" to levy taxes and to allot tax revenue without the colonists' participation in the process was decreed unacceptable, it seemed equally wrong to the unionists in Brand's Hall in 1905 to have the wealth they produced at their jobs taken from them and distributed without the involvement of their elected representatives.

Whatever the history of the advocates of the liberation of work, however, the future of the concept is at present undetermined. Even if democratization of our hours of employment were to become the focus of a movement as large as the present feminist movement, or as small but effective as the I.W.W. in its first years, the specifics of such democratization are by no means settled.

Three times in the twentieth century major attempts were made to extend democracy to the workplace throughout a society as an integral part of a larger democratization of community life. Unfortunately two of these attempts were undertaken in the midst of civil wars. In Ukraine, the insurgency of Nestor Mahkno and his compatriots—fighting against both the Whites and the Reds between 1918 and 1921—included the establishment and protection of rural agricultural communes and urban workers' self-management of enterprises in areas under Mahknovist control (Arshinov passim). In Spain fifteen years later, primarily in rural Aragon and more urbanized Catalonia (Barcelona in particular), between 1936 and 1939 rural agricultural communes and worker management of industries were instituted and thrived until the defeat of the Spanish Republic by Franco's armies, assisted by the military of Fascist Italy and Nazi Germany (Dolgoff passim). On a different scale, the rise of the Polish free trade union Solidarity for fifteen months beginning in August of 1980 led to experimentation with self-management by city workers and farmers (Persky and Flam passim, especially 177-240). These developments took place in an atmosphere of intense hostility on the part of the ruling Communist Party of Poland. And once again, this social experimentation was crushed by the military when on December 13, 1981 Party head Gen. Wojciech Jaruzelski formally declared "a state of war" and imposed martial law (Persky and Flam 14).

Civil war of course distorted such attempts in the last century to try out what democratization of daily work for a whole society might be like in practice. Anyone interested in a future for this concept, though, must carefully examine such earlier struggles. Even allowing for the problems of functioning in a wartime or police-state atmosphere, certain difficulties with implementing workplace freedom emerge.

First is the matter of investment: any new enterprise requires money up front to start, and enterprises that are already operating often require infusions of money in order to modernize or expand. Who controls a community's pool of investment money? How is such a pool accumulated, distributed, regulated, refilled by users? On a smaller scale, if I want to invest in an enterprise (whether on a face-to-face basis, or through purchase of stocks or shares), how can I be sure my investment is protected? Can I reasonably expect some return on my investment? What is an acceptable rate of return, and who or what determines this?

Related to this question of the formation and distribution of capital is the issue of innovation. How can a society be certain that new products and services, and improvements to existing ones, will be funded adequately to ensure their appearance? This problem is linked to the role of the marketplace, including the functions of advertising, consumer protection, environmental protection, prevention of monopolies.

Other questions include whether there is a place for trade unions in a self-managed enterprise. And who or what adjudicates competing needs, such as when the self-managed suppliers of a raw material require a price increase to stay economically viable, but a self-managed factory that uses the raw material cannot remain solvent if they pay the increase? Also, how does self-management of individual enterprises permit the implementation of community or regional or even national industrial strategies?

Speaking of nations, what is the relation between employee-controlled businesses and services, and governments at all levels? Here is how one group within Polish Solidarity tried to clarify roles in their own precarious—and ultimately doomed—situation:

> A socialized enterprise is one controlled by self-management. The central authority is a workers' council elected by the whole staff with the right to make decisions concerning the enterprise's most important business. A manager is appointed by the council in a contested election and is responsible to it alone. The enterprise is communal property managed by the workers' council. The influence of centralized state control on the enterprise's activities is exerted by means of economic instruments such as taxes, custom duties, credits and state agreements, as well as by general norms of law such as those concerning environmental protection, technological standards, industrial health and safety, etc. (Persky and Flam 178-9).

When we move to consider the actual people who must implement workplace democracy, other difficulties emerge. Generations of unfreedom have damaged many of us. As a coping technique, we have adopted on- and off-the-job drug addiction (including alcohol, nicotine and caffeine), gambling, theft, fear of responsibility, victimhood and blaming as a response to crisis, suppression of curiosity, substitution of consumption for personal creativity, and other negative behaviours. How can a beneficial new society be constructed if many of the builders are permanently injured in these ways by what they have already endured under the old regime?

Besides the hurtful behavioural legacies of the undemocratic workplace, there is the problem that my right to freedom on the job interferes with your freedom to start a company and do with it—and its employees—anything you want. Abraham Lincoln noted this apparent contradiction in April 1864, in connection with the issue of slavery.

> We all declare for liberty; but in using the same *word* we do not all mean the same *thing*. With some the word liberty may mean for each man to do as he pleases with himself, and the product of his labour; while with others the same may mean for some men to do as they please with other men, and the product of other men's labour. Here are two, not only different, but incompatible things, called by the same name—liberty. … The shepherd drives the wolf from the sheep's throat, for which the sheep thanks the shepherd as a *liberator*, while the wolf denounces him for the same act as the destroyer of liberty. … Hence we behold the processes by which thousands are daily passing from under the yoke of bondage, hailed by some as the advance of liberty, and bewailed by others as the destruction of all liberty. (McPherson 10)

I do not believe these problems posed by workplace democracy are insurmountable. A similar list of problems posed by the lack of freedom at work would appear equally intimidating, and yet we have staggered along under this form of workplace organization for hundreds of years. I fear the silence around work more than I fear the difficulties raised by democracy on the job. That is why I am cheered by the appearance, even on a very small scale, of the new insider's writing about daily work. I'll close by considering briefly some implications of the existing taboo for writers especially. I am convinced that literature which overall omits daily work and its effects offers a false portrait of an individual, a community, a nation, rather than presenting anything close to an accurate reflection of a person or a locale or an age. To preserve the taboo against the details of how our lives at work and off the job are shaped by our employment is to impose a limitation on the effectiveness of art to reveal and assess human existence.

To state my beliefs more optimistically, my opinion is that for writers to *include* the work experience as a central topic of literature is to undertake the creation of truly adult art, of adult literature. I attempt to amplify this idea further in the introduction to my 1993 selected poems:

> An imaginary world where we do not work to survive may be an adolescent dream, and may offer a picture of a more beautiful existence than is now an actual possibility for us. But sooner or later a functioning adult must face and make choices that involve work. The alternative is to remain dependent—on luck, chance, friends, relatives, the mercy of those with more power, the state. That is why I believe what I write is the literature of the future: an adult literature. As I stated in my 1983 book of essays, *Inside Job*:
>
>> Just as a child or adolescent often does not understand work or money, so our literature mostly has ignored these and focussed instead on the unlikely lives of those whose day-to-day existence apparently is not governed by concerns of work or money: the rich, killers, outlaws, or fantastic representations of people doing certain real jobs (doctors, cowboys, policemen, and so on).
>>
>> The new work writing takes up the challenge of portraying the world an adult sees and attempts to understand and/or change. A grown person who constantly evades having to cope with reality, who lives in a world of dreams however beautiful, we consider immature if not mentally ill. The contemporary industrial writing provides maturity and a healthy balance to literature.

… This is not to say that an adult poetry must be dreary. … To an adolescent, adulthood may seem a reduced state of being, as responsibilities and commitments limit the boundless possibilities of dream. But to a functioning adult, skills and knowledge gained make possible the creation of a life, not merely the response to it. This sense of strength, of efficacy, of potential power to solve problems that are encountered and thus to tangibly shape the world a better way, move the competent adult out of passiveness into life-enhancing activities that can benefit both the self and the surrounding community.

In any case, every human emotion is part of adult life, that is, of work. Joy, wonder, laughter, games, rebellion, lust, love can be experienced at the jobsite, since work—however undemocratically structured today—is in its last analysis a place where human beings gather to remanufacture the world. Yet every activity found in the shop or office or factory is warped by its occurrence within a more-or-less authoritarian environment, just as our lives are warped by our and our neighbours' daily participation in this environment. We deny this, as a society, at our peril. (13-15)

Creation of an adult literature incorporating an accurate, insider's depiction of our jobs is an urgent necessity. A literary culture that describes and evaluates the core everyday experience of the members of a community would help provide us with a sense of our worth, would help instil self-confidence. In an essay on Canadian culture, I explore why I feel self-confidence is so vital an attribute:

I believe self-confidence is the root of democracy. If I do not consider myself important, why would I think I have the right to participate in determining what happens to me and to my community? Self-confidence on the part of the majority is *necessary* for the maintenance and extension of democracy. Since I consider democracy to be the form of social organization that offers the best chance for creating a fair, equitable and happy society, I regard a culture that promotes self-confidence as a *requirement* for the preservation and enhancement of human dignity.

A culture that diminishes or retards people's self-confidence, either through what it proposes or omits, I believe is a threat to democracy. When what we do and who we are are not considered culturally significant, when our contribution to society is hidden behind "big names" (for example, when a corporate executive is said to "make" the product our labour and imagination help create, or an architect is described as having "built" the building we worked on), then the worth of our lives is diminished compared to the value of a comparatively few other people. It is only a step from this to thinking that a "name" person is more important than we are, and hence that his or her thoughts, activities, opinions, etc. are more worthy and should have more weight than our own. This last idea, of course, is counter to the very basis of democracy.

And if we do not consider our lives important, then it is unlikely we will do much to change our lives for the better. Most movements in history that lead to a deepening and broadening of democracy begin with a belief among the activists that they *deserve* the changes they are battling for. In short, people involved with achieving social change have self-confidence. The barons who confronted King John to obtain the Magna Carta, no less than the men and women who fought for and won the eight-hour day, no less than the women who successfully struggled for the right to vote all had the self-confidence that led them to demand changes that were considered radical, unnatural, impossible to the established wisdom of their day. If Canadian employees are to achieve an extension of democracy to that part of our lives where we do not yet have the right to vote—the workplace— we will need the self-confidence that we *deserve* democracy in every aspect of our social existence. ("Laramie" 25-26)

To conclude on a personal note, I regard the liberation of our working life as a goal worth striving for because attainment of this aim would lead to a better existence for me. Arts grants, a supportive family and other lucky circumstances have occasionally accorded me a space to be free from selling my time and to pursue my art uninterrupted. But I know even during such blessed months that what happens in the workplace intrudes on my life. My observation is that

> [a]rtists sometimes feel they have escaped the cage of daily waged or salaried employment if they can survive economically through selling their art or their artistic knowledge. But … [e]ven if you and I succeed in finding or creating non-hierarchically-managed employment for ourselves, we live surrounded by women and men who do not enjoy this privilege. And it is among these people — including our relatives, children, friends — that we must spend our time on this planet. Not until all are free are any of us disentangled from the undemocratic chains and cables that contemporary work tightens around the members of our community. And we will never build Paradise with slave labour. ("Sitting" 177)

I am convinced that we can make as central in literature as in life the details and effects and consequences of our daily jobs. We can articulate the need for, and act to achieve, democracy at the heart of our day. I want us not to pass on to our children the same conditions of servitude in employment that we and our ancestors have hated and grumbled about and cursed, and that have stunted and twisted our lives in ways that even now we fear to examine closely.

I believe that how daily work is organized at present is not good enough for the free citizens of a democracy. I believe that being free is not a part-time matter, a hobby or luxury we engage in during those hours left over from getting ready to go to work, travelling to and back from our place of employment, working, and recovering physically and/or mentally from our workplace experiences.

I believe freedom is a full-time job.

Works Cited

Arishov, Peter. *History of the Makhnovist Movement.* Trans. Lorraine and Fredy Perlman. Detroit: Black & Red, 1974. Print.

Bartlett, John, ed. *Familiar Quotations.* 13th ed. Boston: Little, Brown, 1955. Print.

Dolgoff, Sam. ed. *The Anarchist Collectives: Workers' Self-management in the Spanish Revolution.* Montreal: Black Rose, 1974. Print.

The Founding Convention of the I.W.W. Stenographic report. New York: Merit, 1969. Print.

McPherson, James M. "Liberating Lincoln." *The New York Review of Books* 41.8 (21 Apr. 1994): 7-10. Print.

Persky, Stan and Henry Flam, eds. *The Solidarity Sourcebook.* Vancouver: New Star, 1982. Print.

Wayman, Tom. *A Country Not Considered: Canada, Culture, Work.* Toronto: Anansi, 1993. Print.

—. "An Aspirin as Big as the Sun: Poetry and Politics." Wayman, *A Country* 111-143.

—. "Introduction: A Country Not Considered." Wayman, *A Country* 1-14.

—. "Introduction: Glad I Was Born." *Did I Miss Anything? Selected Poems 1973-1993* . Madeira Park, B.C.: Harbour, 1993. 11-16. Print.

—. "Laramie or Squamish: What Use is Canadian Culture?" Wayman, *A Country* 15-27.

—. "Sitting by the Grave of Literary Ambition: Where I Am Now in my Writing." Wayman, *A Country* 169-179.

EVERY PAGE
Where We Are with Work Writing

My approach to literature was partially formed by the eruption of folk songs into mainstream pop culture in the late 1950s and early 1960s when I was a teenager. The lyrics and emotional content of the music of folk songs spoke powerfully to me of lives both unlike and like my own, of a sense of membership in a wider community existing across space and time, and of the wonder and terror of being human.

In the traditional folk song or spiritual "All My Trials," one verse constitutes the theme music for my interest in people writing about their own daily employment and its effects on their lives on and off the job, and for my aim to see work take its place as one of the great themes of art along with love, death and nature. "I had a little book was given to me," the song goes, "and every page spelled 'Liberty.'"

At this moment in human history, nowhere on Earth are people free at work. Through enormous effort and bloody struggles lasting centuries, many societies such as our own now offer their citizens a way of functioning we call political democracy. Once a citizen of such a society shows up at work, however, all the rights and advantages available off the job are null and void. As I have written about elsewhere, the office door or factory gate is like a time machine out of some science fiction tale. When we cross through to our employment, we go back to an era when people like ourselves do not yet possess the vote, let alone many of the social privileges and protections we take for granted in our hours away from the job. Our exclusion from structural decision-making at work is a tenacious residue of an age when such decision-making in the larger social fabric was restricted to those who had inherited positions of power and/or who owned land—the land everybody else had to use to make a living. The contemporary workplace, then, is a major part of the social environment not yet colonized by democracy.

So pervasive is the idea that work and democracy are incompatible that even when an enterprise is owned in a political democracy by the public—that is, when the jobsite is the property of the collectivity of supposedly free and democratic citizens—work is organized exactly the same as in private corporations. As employees of either sort of enterprise, our lives are further affected by how we constantly must alternate between hours when we are expected to docilely obey unelected authority, and hours when we are supposed to be free and responsible citizens, spouses, parents and inhabitants of a particular ecosystem. Yet if we are infantilized hour after hour daily at the job, we do not magically transform ourselves into fully-functional adults in the parking lot or at the bus stop at quitting time. This schizophrenic daily shuttle we are forced to endure between two consciousnesses—free/not free; free/not free—cannot help but contribute negatively to our behaviours in every sphere of our off-the-job lives.

This predicament is made worse by a pervasive taboo against an accurate depiction of daily work. This taboo aims to ensure no one admits the existence, and explores the implications, of our lack of freedom on the job. I have noted the absence of any material even touching on work in literature textbooks or literary anthologies that claim to present "the human story." For another example, see Patrick Watson's and Benjamin Barber's 1988 volume *The Struggle For Democracy*, the "companion volume to the CBC/ITV television series" sponsored by Petro-Canada. In 298 pages supposedly exploring democracy's storied past and present contradictions, work is *never mentioned*—except for a few paragraphs on indentured bondsmen in a quarry in India. There is no listing for "work" or "labour" in the volume's index.

Clearly, for me, the latter tome is not the little book whose every page spells "Liberty." For decades my hope has been to find those pages on which freedom is imprinted in the writing about daily work that I have anthologized, promoted, authored myself, and responded to in critical essays.

Not that the lack of jobsite democracy is the only topic of these poems and stories that intrigues me. Where we are employed is a place where human beings gather. Therefore nearly *every* human activity and emotion is found in this literature—as we might expect. My model for work writing is the poems and stories and plays produced in other social struggles for human liberation, from black power to the women's movement. In each of these instances, a wide variety of subjects engaged the attention of authors committed to the cause. The proponents of liberation have stressed that unless we are able to look unflinchingly at our present society, we cannot repair social wrongs, cannot move forward from here. Thus to me all accurate writing about daily work—*whatever* the aspect of the job experience that interests the author—has enormous value in breaking the taboo and beginning the inscription of the word "Liberty" onto the pages of our daily life.

Two hallmarks of accuracy in work writing are, for me, an insider's eye and the presence of humour. These two characteristics are interrelated. An insider's eye is necessary for accuracy because an outsider, no matter how sympathetic, does not see what someone going to the job each day comprehends—this jobsite's specific personalities, good days, bad days, particular forms of employee resistance to the established order, irritants and pleasures of the work process. A skilled author can of course *create* an insider's eye through research, careful listening and/or interviewing, application of imagination, and by having the writer's informants verify the resultant piece of writing.

Humour, meanwhile, is how most of us cope with sources of anxiety, with difficulties we find ourselves in. And our employment provides troubles enough for a wealth of comedy. Yet humour of every kind is born in the space between the usual and the unusual. Only an insider grasps whether a particular incident or personality is usual or unusual for that occupation or jobsite. Outsiders can share the punchline when the tension between the usual and unusual is made plain by the teller of the joke, or when the humour is located between the outsider's expectation of the usual and the joke's revelation of something unexpected.

Overall, my hopes for the work writing have remained undiminished through the decades because when I take the long view of human history I observe that area after area of our common life has been democratized—however slowly and painfully and however circuitous the route to this end. Also, an inborn human trait seems to be that whenever a taboo is established and enforced, men and women sooner or later expose, challenge and obliterate the denial.

I take heart, too, because I have been invited to speak dozens of times about the work writing to groups of high school teachers under various auspices. My talk is invariably met with an acknowledgment of the absence of any significant accurate look at work in the current curriculum. But sometimes a more sophisticated level of understanding is evident.

In September of 1997 I was invited to address a gathering in Rochester, New York of educators and unionists. The Rochester school board, despairing of complaints from employers that high school grads from inner city schools lacked basic skills to hold a job, had instituted a certificate of employability program. Students who, for example, were present in class a high percentage of the time, had a low number of lates, and who demonstrated other behaviours connected with submitting to a routinized life were certified by the schools as fit for employment.

The certificate program sparked the inauguration of a new organization of teachers and union activists called REAL, the Rochester Educational Alliance for Labor. REAL met annually, and produced materials to give a different slant on employment issues than the approved curriculum. What I found impressive was that REAL had quickly identified the heart of the dilemma. The desired qualities one wishes to instil in an *employee*—unquestioning obedience, docility, tractability, limited curiosity about the world immediately around one—are the exact opposite of the qualities one desires in a *citizen* of a democracy—critical thinking, curiosity about one's surroundings, articulateness and creativity, ability and willingness to become involved in community affairs.

Is it the function of our schools to produce employees, or citizens, REAL asked. Surely we do no favours to a child if our curriculum renders them so self-assured, so imbued with the spirit of freedom as to make them unfit or unwilling to obtain a job. And how much more is this an unhelpful outcome if the child is—as many children in Rochester's public school system are—from a family trapped in a generational cycle of unemployment, poverty, welfare. Yet we do no favours to a child either—or to the greater community—if our school curriculum crushes a child's spirits and curiosity, shrinking the manifold possibilities of life into obedience to established hierarchies, punching in on time, and regarding the consumption of certain goods and services as the height and extent of one's dreams and ambitions.

REAL had no easy answers to this impasse. How does one show young people—who can be very absolute in their judgments—how to adopt a double consciousness, the one each of us who successfully hangs onto a job has managed to internalize?

My conviction is that the work writing can help educators explore this conundrum, and my presence in Rochester indicates this belief was shared by members of REAL. And I further would argue that an accurate examination of daily work—with the work writing as part of this process—is necessary to assist in resolving another urgent social issue.

Several years ago the U.S. political theorist Todd Gitlin spoke on CBC radio's "Ideas" program about the paralysis of any effective opposition to triumphant global capital's harmful impact on our lives. He identified the cause of this failure as the disappearance of a commons. When social movements in our history had confronted the undemocratic control over our well-being by governments, corporations or wealthy individuals, such movements were coalitions of people and groups each with wide-ranging agendas. But they were alliances with a sense of *common* purpose, too.

Gitlin had praise for the advances in the status of women, gays and lesbians, minorities, and aboriginals over the past two or three decades, and acknowledged how much more remains to be done to redress past wrongs and improve inherited attitudes. But he pointed out that each group now seeks fulfillment of their albeit-just demands at the *expense* of the commons. Gone is a sense of responsibility to a larger community, let alone a larger community of resistance. The result has been a more divided society, not a more unified one, and a society that has been helpless to stem the increasing reduction of our common quality of life.

A joke circulated on the Internet is a precise echo of Gitlin's point. Of course the tale circulated is intended as *humour*, but humour is how, as I have mentioned, our species deals with tensions and troubles. The joke is a purported series of memos from an enterprise's employee charged with organizing the annual Christmas party. Following the initial memo announcing the event, various interest groups among the company's staff one by one make their demands—based on differing religions, food preferences, alcohol addiction, eating disorders, and many more individual orientations. After each righteous request, a memo announces that the planned party has been duly reconfigured to satisfy the complaint. After several revisions to the original plan, the beleaguered organizer has a mid-memo breakdown, and her replacement cancels the event. Each of the various demands made on the commons is reasonable from the point of view of the interest group requesting the change. But the totality of these demands destroys the opportunity for a gathering together, an opportunity to mutually communicate, celebrate, and potentially enjoy one another's companionship.

I felt Gitlin in his talks failed to identify where a common focal point of resistance might be found. To me, the undone task we all share with others—regardless of gender, race, sexual orientation, mental or physical challenges, etc.—is unquestionably the democratization of work. There is no enduring freedom, no lasting satisfaction in life for any of us as long as our liberty does not extend to the daily workplace. What happens to us there shapes us, shapes our day, shapes the other men and women of our community despite whatever gains we might have achieved and still *should* strive for as members of this or that minority or majority. And an accurate depiction of daily employment in our literature has a vital role to play in helping to demonstrate this commonality.

Why, then, has work writing had so little impact to date on education, literature, society? For I would have to conclude that despite the best efforts of some educators and labour arts enthusiasts, a searching examination of work continues to be mainly absent as a major theme in our school curriculums and in our literature. Work-based anthologies, work writing groups, literary periodicals' theme issues on work arrive and vanish. But with few exceptions, the taboo endures fundamentally intact.

I believe art about work will not attain any centrality in our cultural life until there is a corresponding social movement fighting for the democratization of employment. This belief is based on societal attitudes toward authors who over the centuries portrayed the condition of women. Only once the battle for women's emancipation emerged from the shadows to engage the mainstream of our culture did these "lost" authors became known and read and honoured. But in a society that cloaked women's lives in taboo, such authors and their books were interesting or irrelevant footnotes to the main cultural business-as-usual of their time.

Work writing will continue to lack a significant audience in a society such as ours as long as the chief role of the entertainment media—which now includes what used to be called the news and arts sectors—is to lead people *away* from paying attention to their own actual working lives. This effect is largely reinforced by our educational system.

Moreover, the union movement in North America has, in part due to the Cold War, mostly abandoned any social change component. Yet the philosophical *basis* for unionism's existence is the right to be a fully functional human being on the job as well as off, to obtain control over the manifold dimensions of how the job impacts your life—in short, to extend democracy to the workplace. Our present business unions, however, have little interest in the struggle to ultimately free our lives from being subjected to the decisions of an unelected hierarchy of power. In place of such a struggle, such unions offer an attempt to ameliorate the conditions of our servitude. This vision of unionism has proven to be no match for inflation, globalization, legislated wage controls, incessant anti-union propaganda and the rise of a social climate that passively witnesses the deindustrialization of communities and the nation, and that permits executives to enjoy remuneration hundreds of times greater than their employees. As a result, union members have steadily lost ground with regard to real wages and workplace rights, while the union movement itself has steadily shrunk.

Based on my years on this planet, I have concluded that enduring, beneficial social change is made by men and women with the self-confidence to feel they *deserve* a better life. Oppression alone seldom provokes more than short-lived revolt. And the self-confidence necessary to accomplish change arises, I believe, from a sense of hope, and a sense of pride. At present, the hopes of a majority of Canadians reside not with any collective action to improve their lives along with those of their neighbours. Hope is pretty much restricted to winning the lottery. Pride seems to be located in people's responses to corporatized sports teams, or in the attainment of good deals while shopping.

Canadians have been convinced their contribution to their community consists not of their work—their creation of objects or services intended to be useful to their fellow citizens—but rather is a result of the consumption of things. In this mind-set, the only acceptable form of social transformation is via *products*—the possession of certain consumer goods, and access to certain services. Thus we have the computer revolution or the wireless digital revolution or a fashion revolution. The most highly valued contribution an individual can make to her or his country is to become a product herself or himself—a celebrity whose presence can be sold for the biggest possible price, and who in turn can increase sales for products she or he is associated with. Yet the work we each do can potentially be a source of pride. And, in concert with the aspirations of others, our jobs that reconstruct society each day can potentially be a source of hope to fashion a better community, a better life for each of us.

Obviously, the project of the liberation of work faces enormous obstacles such as the ones I have touched on here. Yet I am not discouraged about freedom's eventual victory, nor about art's potential contribution to that transformative event. While work literature in our society has not moved any closer to taking its delights and information and alternative vision to centre stage, neither has work writing vanished or even diminished in the past decades.

Working remains a subversive act because the conditions of our employment give the lie both to the claims of the state concerning the triumph of democracy, and to the claims of commercial advertising concerning the attainment of self-worth. Members of our species have always sought the truth, no matter how circuitous the route to it, or how obscured the truth is in a social structure. Hence work writing that portrays even a small part of the realities of the job will survive on society's margins. The continued existence of work literature mirrors the way folk music endures during periods when people view themselves as isolated individuals rather than as men and women who draw strength from and have a responsibility toward some larger whole. This connection with others, which the work writing illuminates so vividly, is the only road to freedom, to each of us truly acquiring that little book with "Liberty" upon every page.

AGAINST THE SMILING BASTARDS

And you, to whom adversity has dealt the final blow
With smiling bastards lying to you everywhere you go,
Turn to, and put out all your strength of arm and heart and brain
And, like the Mary Ellen Carter, rise again.
—Stan Rogers, "The Mary Ellen Carter"

I n Canada during the twentieth century, only two postsecondary
institutions were entirely closed by governments. Both of these were
in Nelson, B.C.

Nelson is a town of 10,000 perched on a mountainside where the
West Arm of Kootenay Lake shrinks to assume again the designation
of Kootenay River. The habitation, surrounded by the peaks of the
southern Selkirks, is an eight-hour drive west of Calgary, a nine-and-
a-half-hour drive east of Vancouver, and a fifty-minute drive north
from the U.S. border. As if reflecting something of the town's setting,
Nelson's citizens have proven to be rock-solid about at least two things:
a determination to be a centre for postsecondary education, and an
unshakable belief in the importance of the arts. These two convictions

have led to the creation of two innovative schools that I am proud to have been associated with: the Kootenay School of Writing in the 1980s and the Kootenay School of the Arts in the 1990s.

Naturally, the passionate belief in education and the arts is not held equally among Nelson's mixed population of citizens engaged in resource extraction, government services, tourism, light manufacturing and the hundred varieties of small-town commerce from law firms to purveyors of agricultural supplies. Also in the population mix are ski- and snowboard-bums, dope growers, equity refugees from urban real estate booms, retirees, and several successive waves of back-to-the-landers from Doukhobors who settled in the region in the 1910s to contemporary ecology freaks. But enough townsfolk are convinced of the importance of education and the arts to make Nelson, despite forty years of setbacks, a model for activism on behalf of these pursuits.

The first postsecondary institution that a twentieth century government shut down completely was Notre Dame University of Nelson, in 1977. The university had begun in the 1950s as the vision of a priest fishing in the West Arm, glancing up to see rising on a bench above Fairview, the easternmost district of Nelson, a Catholic college to train clergymen. For financial reasons, the diocese increasingly over the years turned to the provincial government for funding. But the spirit of Notre Dame—and the physical construction of many campus buildings still in use—was very much a community undertaking. In its more secular latter days, Notre Dame achieved distinction as the first Canadian university to offer sports scholarships—Olympic skier Nancy Greene was a product of NDU's lively sports program. And Notre Dame faculty were the first in the province to defy a legislated prohibition against unionization of postsecondary faculty. Their willingness to organize themselves despite the law blazed the trail for the nearly 100 per cent faculty unionization of B.C.'s public postsecondary institutions today.

When B.C.'s Social Credit government announced the closure of NDU in 1977, claiming financial reasons, the town, outraged, fought back with an array of protests and petitions. In response to the storm of opposition, in 1979 a new venture opened in the slightly-refurbished halls of NDU: David Thompson University Centre. DTUC was a consortium of the University of Victoria and of Selkirk College in Castlegar, forty kilometres southwest of Nelson. The latter institution was inaugurated in 1966 as one of the two-year community colleges intended to relieve enrolment pressure on the province's universities.

At DTUC, students could obtain a four-year BA under UVic's auspices. In many ways, DTUC was a trial run for what would be known later in B.C. as "university colleges"—essentially two-year colleges permitted to provide four years of instruction and grant degrees in certain areas of study.

Among the unique offerings at DTUC was a rural education program, to prepare teachers to serve in non-urban districts. This program recognized for the first time that the demands on teachers in smaller communities are significantly different than on those working in the anonymity of larger urban centres—where all the province's teacher training occurred before DTUC existed. DTUC also incorporated a longstanding Nelson community institution, the Kootenay School of Art (note the singular designation of "Art"), which was merged with DTUC to become its Fine Arts department. KSA, like NDU, had begun in the 1950s as a community initiative, and from 1969 to 1977 KSA students could earn a BEd or BFA degree by taking their required academic courses at NDU and their arts courses at KSA.

DTUC also included a vibrant writing program, begun under the direction of poet and former Selkirk College instructor Fred Wah. Wah was partly raised in the area, as he describes in his prose memoir *Diamond Grill*, and later he was awarded the 1985 Governor General's Literary Award for Poetry and served as Canada's fifth Parliamentary Poet Laureate 2011-2013. At DTUC he assembled a faculty that included over the years GG winners Paulette Giles and John Newlove, as well as respected authors such as David McFadden, Sean Virgo, Colin Browne. Wah tirelessly pushed the limits of the possible—he insisted students become familiar with personal computers, a novelty in 1979. He founded the boundary-challenging literary magazine *Writing*, and—recognizing from his own experience what it was like to grow up in an isolated mountain valley—conducted annual field trips of writing students to Vancouver and/or Toronto so participants could meet first hand with many of the nation's premiere editors, publishers and authors. I was hired to teach writing and journalism at DTUC from 1980 to 1982. The place had a do-it-yourself spirit I enjoyed, where there were no limits to imaginative pedagogy except the energy of oneself and one's colleagues.

DTUC foundered on the rock of the province-wide public sector general strike of autumn 1983. Briefly, that spring the Social Credit government of Bill Bennett had introduced a budget featuring draconian cuts to every aspect of the public service. Led by the B.C. Federation of Labour, and nudged constantly forward by ad hoc community groups like Women Against the Budget, a loose coalition of the province's citizenry dubbed Operation Solidarity resisted the implementation of the Bennett budget.

These were heady days for me, now back living in Vancouver and teaching for Kwantlen College in Surrey, B.C. I had long been a believer—following the ideas of the Industrial Workers of the World, with whose Vancouver General Membership Branch I was currently active—that the general strike represents the only effective non-violent route to a reorganization of society in order to introduce democracy to those hours we are employed, and to recognize the effect on the larger community of the goods and services our workplaces produce. If the people whose daily work reproduces the world simply don't show up, or if they begin as part of a general strike at their jobs to recreate the world in a new way, then effective changes become possible without revolutionary bloodshed. Once the population recognizes their value to the community as *producers*, rather than consumers, then society's parasites—from politicians to whatever entertainment or sports celebrities the media promotes at the moment as society's significant individuals—are revealed as the essentially useless figures they are.

While Operation Solidarity gathered steam over the summer, Vancouver seemed a city transformed. At community meeting after community meeting I attended, every idea seemed up for grabs. People rose from the floor to question the roles of politicians of all stripes, of management, of the media, of the educational system, of unions themselves. A high point for me was a rally at Empire Stadium, where before packed stands of demonstrators a parade of union representatives marched onto the field led by … the Vancouver Police pipe band. For the wages of peace officers, no less than teachers, ferry workers and garbage collectors, was threatened by the pay freeze contained in the new budget. And the impact of cuts to hospitals, educational facilities, libraries and other public services affected peace officers the same as any other citizen. What became clear to all within earshot of the police bagpipes was that without the police and legal system's willingness to club, shoot, jail, or otherwise cow ordinary people into submission, the ability of "elected representatives" or bosses to direct society would be nonexistent. The people whose work feeds, clothes, houses, teaches, transports and heals their fellow citizens would be free to establish a community with different goals, perhaps, than immense private gains for a few at the cost of ruthless economic exploitation of the natural and human environment.

Since the provincial government refused to compromise on their budget, the B.C. Fed adopted an escalating general strike beginning in October as the centrepiece of the fightback campaign. The mainstream unions' ambivalence concerning this plan was evident in many ways, not least their decision to have the teachers' union kick off the strike. Unions representing other components of the public service were to join the strike every few days, according to a pre-established timetable. Labour insiders said that by picking the conservative teachers to initiate the strike, the B.C. Fed leadership was hoping for a failure to honour picket lines, which would be their excuse for abandoning the escalating general strike tactic in favour of something less challenging to the status quo. Already the public mood of questioning everything was seen as threatening to the business unionism represented by the B.C. Fed. This type of unionism has abandoned advocacy of fundamental social change, change that is integral to unionism's rationale. Instead, business unionism is content to serve as a labour broker, selling the work of its membership at the highest possible price but never seeking to alter the master/servant relationship of bosses and employees established during the Industrial Revolution.

The B.C. Fed leadership had not counted on the women. On the first day of the strike, Women Against the Budget organized neighbourhood groups to picket every school. School support staff, who were scheduled to keep working even though teachers struck, refused to cross the lines of parents and school neighbours carrying picket signs. Many teachers who might have crossed through to work also thought better of it. The strike was on. When college teachers went out a few days later, we at Kwantlen met virtually every day to reconsider our participation in the expanding general strike. Always some Kwantlen business instructors would argue legalities and moralities at our meeting in their opposition to our bargaining unit's continued participation. A few business faculty resigned from the union, and even crossed our line. But with few students to teach, and no other classes for those students who insisted on entering the empty college buildings, these actions by individuals opposed to the strike were more symbolic than anything else. The faculty vote each day to continue to strike was overwhelmingly in favour.

B.C. society was transformed. On picket lines, in union or community meetings, or casual encounters of all sorts, people did not talk about the latest TV shows, sports, or any other public spectacles designed to divert our attention from considering the facts of our everyday lives. Instead, conversation was about the implications of what we were doing, and about imagining new means of organizing society other than what we have been given. The B.C. political party that usually poses as the "opposition," the NDP, evaporated as a functional entity—issuing no comments either for or against the general strike, and deserted by its street-level activists who instead adopted a more direct means to confront the social situation.

The media, meantime, focused as hard as they could on strike-breakers, attempting to generate the impression of a collapse of the strike. But, relentlessly, in accordance with the B.C. Fed's timetable, unit after unit of the public sector hit the bricks despite—at least on the Lower Mainland—October's usual steady downpour. In an atmosphere that foreshadowed the collapse of the Soviet Union, when the usually-willing-to-obey cease being obedient, the hollowness of legislatures, parliaments and political parties was revealed. Power was shifting elsewhere. Even the media began to be circumvented, as people reported by telephone to friends in other parts of the province the success of the strike in their own locales—Prince George, Quesnel, and, yes, Nelson. Outside Kamloops, a residential mental health institution, Tranquille, was occupied by its workers rather than be placed behind picket lines. Management was run off the jobsite, and the Operation Solidarity flag flew over the buildings.

With the final public sector components about to go out, the B.C. Federation of Labour succumbed to panic. The Fed leadership perhaps was terrified that in the new society that was trembling to be born there would be no place for professional union hacks—whatever role unions had in employee- or community-managed enterprises. In any event, the Fed leadership turned to the Woodworkers' right-wing leader Jack Munro to bail them out of the opposition to the budget they had created. On a rainy weekend, two weeks after the start of the strike, with picket lines standing firm across the province, Munro was whisked away by government jet to Kelowna to meet with the premier. The two men emerged from a meeting to announce the strike was over. Strikers were to return to work Monday without a vote. In return, the strikers would get, er, nothing. The media quickly dubbed this "The Kelowna Accord" and their praise for Munro's "statesmanship" rang to the skies.

The government's vengeance was swift. In Nelson just prior to the strike, DTUC had been assessed by a blue-ribbon government committee and pronounced a success. DTUC's future thus was supposedly assured for at least a further five years, after which the next review would be undertaken. On the heels of the sellout of the general strike, however, the B.C. government announced DTUC would be closed May 1, 1984. Many locals believed this was the area's payback not only for being particularly strong in support of the strike, but also for having earlier re-elected an NDP MLA.

If I have dwelt at length on what participation in the 1983 provincial public sector general strike felt like, I have done so because the energy that propelled the creation of the Kootenay School of Writing and, subsequently, the Kootenay School of the Arts was a direct consequence of the social potential that the autumn of 1983 revealed to many people in B.C. The anarchists have a saying: "There is a mountain locked up in everyday life, that from time to time is revealed." Some of us were determined not to let the mountain subside.

First, though, we had to endure the closing of DTUC. I was hired in January jointly by the faculty association and the student government to establish a media centre for the battle against DTUC's closure, and to train students to staff the centre. I resigned from Kwantlen and drove east back to Nelson to begin.

Years later I recognized in the lyrics of folksinger-songwriter Stan Rogers' song, "The Mary Ellen Carter," the spirit of the struggle to keep DTUC alive. Rogers' song concerns a group of sailors dismissed once their ship is sunk due to the ineptitude of its officers. The seamen are determined to salvage the written-off vessel, to "make the Mary Ellen Carter rise again." A similar resolve was how many faculty and students felt about preventing the loss of the educational experiment that was DTUC, the school into whose existence we had poured our imagination, time, energy. The goal in the soon-bustling media centre, and for dozens of protest initiatives was, as Rogers states, to try to make what had been taken from us

> *Rise again, rise again, that her name not be lost*
> *To the knowledge of men.*
> *All those who loved her best and were with her till the end*
> *Will make the Mary Ellen Carter rise again.*

It's easy to say that a school—or an industrial plant—"closes." The difficulty is to communicate the human cost of deindustrialization or the removal of any other community asset like a school. We of the fightback campaign issued the usual press releases, and organized the expected community rallies, including protest trips to Victoria. But DTUC Photography Dept. head Jeremy Addington photographed every DTUC employee scheduled to lose her or his job on May 1. Many were portrayed grouped with their families. Addington mounted the photos in a room-sized display, and under each portrait was a brief statement by the picture's subject or subjects about what DTUC, and/or losing their employment, meant to them. The wall of depictions of those affected by the end of DTUC was a powerful artwork that never failed to move viewers. Thereafter, those who had seen the display understood emotionally, not just intellectually, what the abrupt end of an enterprise means to the human beings displaced.

Despite all our efforts, the buildings were padlocked on May 1. You could walk up to a campus window and peer in, looking at writing still on a classroom blackboard as though a prof had temporarily put down the chalk and would resume the lesson at the next class. Except there were to be no more classes. The experience of staring in the windows was like that of a diver underwater peering through a porthole at the interior of a sunken ship.

Some of us, however, were determined to salvage what we could from the betrayal of the general strike and, more specifically, from the wreck of DTUC. I'll confess that rage was a factor in our resolve to continue to oppose the will of the men and women whom Rogers' song calls "the laughing, drunken rats who left her to a sorry grave." Some DTUC faculty and staff with seniority at Selkirk College resumed working for their previous employer. Other faculty and many students relocated to the Lower Mainland.

In Vancouver, former DTUC Writing Dept. head Colin Browne (who subsequently taught film-making at Simon Fraser University) convened a meeting of a group of us who had been associated with the Nelson writing program and broached the idea of continuing—and improving—the creative writing curriculum created over five years at DTUC. Browne and I had been faculty, and the others had been students at the institution, including Calvin Wharton (now an author who teaches writing at New Westminster's Douglas College), Jeff Derksen (now an author who teaches at Simon Fraser University), and Gary Whitehead (who subsequently published a short fiction collection). Thus what we called the Vancouver Centre of the Kootenay School of Writing was born.

Meanwhile in Nelson, another branch of KSW formed, which survived until 2012 as a writers' circle sponsoring public readings by authors at the Municipal Library. As well, a group of profs from DTUC's academic program formed the Nelson University Centre, a society which sponsored lectures and academic courses and has lobbied continuously for the return of a liberal arts university to the town. NUC also eventually took custody of the former NDU/DTUC library. A sit-in by seniors that lasted 96 days saved the library when rumours swept through Nelson after DTUC's closure that the library was scheduled to be packed up and transported either to Selkirk College or the University of Victoria. Meantime, even the DTUC Student Society refused to disappear. A group of students' union activists sold community memberships in their organization, and reconstituted themselves as "the world's largest student society without a university." For many years the Student Society operated the former NDU/DTUC Student Union Building as a pub and site for community classes and events.

In Vancouver, the Kootenay School of Writing, operating from a suite of second-story offices we found at Broadway and Oak, offered its first slate of evening classes in September 1984. The School was soon a busy place in the evenings. Browne continually challenged us not to merely reproduce what we had created in Nelson, but to offer educational opportunities for writers and would-be writers that went beyond the standard, lock-step program of 13-week courses—although we offered lots of those in introductory and advanced poetry, fiction, journalism, and more. Writers' talks, weekend courses, week-long master classes were also part of the KSW mix.

Although many of the core administrative group were interested in the latest developments in non-narrative writing, Browne believed that contemporary literature consisted of "many musics." He argued that just as musicians of any tradition can learn from practitioners of other kinds of music, so KSW should embrace and teach as wide a range of writing as possible. In the summer of 1985, we convened in rented space at the Emily Carr art school on Granville Island the first-ever Canadian gathering of the abstruse writers originally gathered around the journal $L=A=N=G=U=A=G=E$. These still-controversial authors were little known in this country at the time we invited them to Vancouver. The following year, KSW co-sponsored the first-ever-anywhere colloquium of work-based writers. The 1986 conference assembled at Trout Lake Community Centre in East Vancouver a spectrum of authors ranging from a group around San Francisco's *Processed World* magazine, who declared all work boring and stupid, to poets like Burnaby carpenter Kate Braid and Boston electrician Susan Eisenberg who were active in the women-in-trades movement, where their occupation was an honoured part of their self-definition.

One day a couple of recent graduates of Emily Carr's curatorial program showed up at KSW, and pointed out that our office and classroom spaces were usually empty during the day. They wanted to launch their own exhibition space, and convinced us this would complement our writing curriculum. Thus Vancouver's Artspeak Gallery began.

All this was done on a shoestring. Our core administrative group survived personally on welfare, unemployment insurance, occasional short-term jobs, and grants. As a group, KSW was successful at applying for Canada Council Explorations support, used to employ KSW core people—albeit at very low wages—for various projects we undertook, and to cover office rent. Eventually the Explorations officer responsible for Western Canada asked us to stop applying and give other folks a chance. The Artspeak Gallery curators suggested we should apply for Council support as an artist-run centre—a program previously limited to the fine arts. Vancouver KSW duly became the first *literary* artist-run centre in the nation.

Though exciting, the years we devoted to keeping KSW not only afloat but churning full steam ahead into uncharted waters began to take their toll. The core administrative group met every Friday afternoon for more than three years to consider every possible problem the fledgling operation encountered—from curriculum planning to the state of seminar tables to janitorial issues like the need to purchase more toilet paper. The weekly meeting could be raucous: it was not unheard of for people to climb up and stand on the table to make a point. At Browne's urging, we continually sought new approaches to problems, from bringing in an architect to look at rearranging our offices to better utilize the small space, to sessions where Browne asked us to consider where we saw KSW, and our own participation in it, in one year, two years, five years. Whether the weekly meeting was jolly or argumentative, though, we each inevitably took away from it a daunting list of chores. Yet the rush of bringing KSW to life, and our pride in KSW's accomplishments, made the work seem worth the stress for quite a while.

By 1987, burnout began to appear among the core group. People began to be snarky on the phone with prospective students, even though students were our lifeblood, our raison d'être. I recall poring over financial accounts in the office late one evening, trying to reconcile some balances, while in an adjacent classroom Browne toiled to complete a grant application. Suddenly I heard a bellow from the room next door: "What has any of this to do with *poetry?*" And I remember a morning in the office when somebody observed that if a donor walked in and handed us a cheque for a million dollars, one of us would complain about having to take on the additional task of carrying the cheque across the street to the bank.

After three and a half years, we decided to end the project of carrying on DTUC's educational legacy in this manner. Following a number of subsequent downsizings and reorganizations, KSW in Vancouver exists today in name only, as a writing circle dedicated to advancing a single narrow component of Browne's "many musics." KSW's name is retained because at the time of the school's dissolution we had obtained federal government status as an educational non-profit organization, permitting financial contributors to obtain a charitable donation receipt for income tax purposes.

In Nelson the dream of salvaging a postsecondary institution continued to be kept alive by several community organizations, among them a DTUC Support Society that dated back to the heyday of that enterprise and which had never disbanded. In 1990, the Society decided that whereas another full-scale university was probably an impossibility, a niche institution focused on the arts might well fly. The decision was made to resurrect the Kootenay School of Art, this time in the plural. The Kootenay School of the Arts, directed by local potter David Lawson, began offering classes in scattered locations across town in September 1991. The Nelson municipal government donated rooms in the tower of the heritage City Hall building for the new KSA's administrative offices.

By this time I had returned to the West Kootenays and purchased an acreage some distance west of Nelson. Determined to have writing be on board the nascent art school, I offered to teach a class under the auspices of the new KSA. In an article I wrote for the *Toronto Star* that appeared in 1992, I reported: "Every Wednesday this winter I get into my truck and drive 60 kilometres over the snowy roads from my mountain home into Nelson, B.C. The purpose of my weekly trip is to teach a university-level introductory course in writing. Despite my deeply-held adherence to, and active participation in, faculty unionism, I conduct this class for the princely sum of $75 a week. With absolutely no benefits. I do this for one reason: love." What I didn't tell the *Star*'s readers was, as I've mentioned above, anger at our losses contributed to my motivation as well.

In October 1991, the NDP won the provincial election; newly-elected NDP MLA Corky Evans had campaigned on a promise to return postsecondary education to Nelson. Over the subsequent years, Evans was almost as good as his word. Once the idea of KSA was endorsed by the province through Evans' efforts, the Nelson municipal government agreed to lease the fledgling institution a large downtown granite fieldstone heritage building, only part of which was in use as an electrical substation. Federal, provincial, municipal and borrowed monies permitted the conversion of the building into studio, office and teaching space for KSA's rapidly expanding offerings. Besides a range of popular community courses, KSA began to offer a full-time credit program starting in September 1994, partially in the refurbished building (finished in 1996) but also in other, rented locations around town.

Evans could never convince the NDP government to charter the school, which would have made it eligible for regular provincial postsecondary funding. But he and school head Lawson convinced the politicians in Victoria of the school's usefulness by pointing out that

B.C. could never support an Ikea-type furniture company, based on our abundant supply of wood and wood-derivative building materials, because Canada lacks any place where imaginative wood furniture design is taught. Eventually a $1 million provincial grant endowed a chair in wood product design at KSA.

Besides this area of study, six other departments, or "Studios" as KSA termed them, served about 120 full-time students and about the same number of part-time and community course enrollees. Clay, Mixed Media (drawing and painting, art history, professional practices), Fibre, Jewellery, Metal and Writing offered first a one-year, then a two-year program. Although KSA was technically a community-owned private non-profit institution, MLA Evans finessed, starting in 1995, an annual lump-sum payment of $400,000 from provincial funds. Essentially, this money was put in a brown paper bag and pushed across a table toward KSA by a broomstick wielded by officials of Emily Carr, who looked the other direction while doing so, whistling a tune. When Emily Carr's accountants eventually balked at the irregularity of funnelling KSA's money through their books in this manner, Selkirk College agreed to assume the chore.

KSA students were about half from the local area, a quarter from southern Alberta, and a quarter from the balance of B.C. and the nation. The faculty, who even at the peak of the institution's life received only about one-third the going rate of community college faculty remuneration, were idealists to a man or woman. All were practicing artists in their field of instruction. And whether or not faculty had a previous connection to DTUC—as former instructors or graduates—all cheerfully worked incredibly long hours keeping KSA functioning. Besides developing and implementing curriculum, KSA faculty—as at KSW—had to build walls and chalkboards, sweep floors, repair equipment and furniture, unclog toilets, counsel students, recruit prospective students, price needed goods and services, prepare budgets, attend endless meetings, and much, much more.

Eventually the school hired a sole maintenance miracle-worker, Nick Jones, whose unstinting efforts in three different KSA teaching locations across Nelson, "patched her rents, stopped her vents, dogged hatch and porthole down. / Put cables to her fore and aft, and girded her around," in the words of Stan Rogers' song. Yet even such heroic service, also significantly underpaid compared to local tradesperson's rates, could not lighten faculty's extracurricular load. In Writing, for example, we established a computer lab with begged, borrowed, and scrounged computers, and launched a Graphic Communications program which demanded we acquire by hook or crook top-end equipment in order to be up-to-date with the rapidly changing technology. Each expansion of curriculum in this way involved many hours of physical labour on the part of faculty to prepare or refurbish classroom space to accommodate the changes.

The rock that holed KSA was mismanagement. On paper, the school was controlled by a community board of governors, quixotically called a Round Table, that included token student and faculty representation. The board was ideologically committed to governing by consensus. As anyone who has been subject to that decision-making technique knows, it is a great means for determining pizza toppings, but completely fails when a group contains fundamentally conflicting interests. And the board's focus of attention increasingly diverged from the very real needs and concerns of faculty members conducting the actual business of the school on a daily basis.

At a certain point, founding director Lawson resigned to head up the Clay Studio, and the board made the fatal mistake of hiring a series of directors whose experience lay in government-funded regular postsecondary educational systems. None of the people at KSA's helm ever grasped the essentially entrepreneurial nature of the KSA venture, nor were any capable of recognizing the incredible amount of unpaid work faculty and staff contributed each day to keep the school under way and on course.

How bad was management? Our band of forty paid-part-time-but-frequently-full-time-on-the-job KSA instructors and support staff finally unionized—an amazing event, given that the backgrounds of most faculty were the art world, not the teaching profession. Only three or four of us had previous experience in working—let alone teaching—in a unionized environment.

One truism of union formation is that the boss is the best organizer, and this proved correct at KSA. Not only were faculty and staff
increasingly resentful of the low pay and endless hours and lack of board
appreciation of their contribution to the school. One evening while
organizing was underway, two management representatives went to
the home of one of the office employees. Standing on the employee's
doorstep in the chilly autumn evening dark, they handed her a letter
terminating her and demanded she surrender her keys to the administration office—in effect, firing her in front of her family. The last
faculty holdouts signed up in the union immediately afterward.

We were enormously assisted in our union drive by the B.C. college
teachers' union central, who gave us a skilled and imaginative staff
representative to lead us through the intricacies of obtaining legal recognition as a bargaining unit, and then hammering out from scratch
a first contract that preserved many of the aspects of self-rule that
Studios enjoyed. Former director Lawson also was a vital asset to the
union, since he knew better than his successors all the inside mech-
anisms of how the school ran. I served as the founding president of
the KSA local, and subsequently over the years was the local secretary,
and twice a member of our bargaining committee.

Management ineptitude reached its height in the run-up to the
provincial election in May 2001 that saw the Socreds under Gordon
Campbell return to power—now calling themselves "Liberals." Nearly
a year before, MLA Evans had called a meeting of KSA board, management and union reps, and correctly predicted that not only would
the NDP lose the next election, but that Campbell would cut off KSA's
annual provincial stipend. Since Evans deemed it impossible to press
the NDP cabinet before their demise to charter KSA as a regularly
funded provincial institution, he urged KSA to seek affiliation with
an existing provincially funded postsecondary school.

His suggestion was one the union had for some years been urging
KSA's board to undertake. We had faced the fact that the nickel-and-
dime financial condition of the institution—a situation we realized
was an inevitable consequence of its oddball status—could not be
offset in the long haul even by the dedicated (and largely unpaid)

work of its faculty and staff. Faculty continued to see a tremendous potential for the school, but this was a future that clearly could not be realized without a infusion of stable funding.

Management, however, either could not or would not act on Evans' suggestion. When the blow fell in Spring 2002, management was faced with relying henceforth solely on tuition to fund the school. Their response was to immediately fire the two Studios, Mixed Media and Writing, who boasted some of the largest enrolments among the school's seven areas of study. Subsequently, Wood Product Design was also axed, and Metal ordered to jettison its second-year program. As the breadth of the school's offerings shrank, enrolment plummeted along with the morale and volunteer spirit of faculty and staff. On July 1, 2006, half a decade too late, control of the remaining shell of KSA was formally transferred to Selkirk College. Twenty full-time students enrolled as the incoming class for 2006-2007. This compares to twenty-five students who signed on in 1994, when KSA first began to offer full-time credit studies twelve years before. And KSA has continued to suffer from life-threatening enrolment numbers, since the health of the institution has never been a priority of its present overseers at Selkirk.

Although KSA intermittently circles the drain, Nelson remains Nelson. The two terminated Studios, without missing a beat, formed the Nelson Fine Arts Centre in 2002 to continue to offer as much of the programming as possible that they had provided when components of KSA. I was involved in the initial planning and implementation committee that saw NFAC into existence, before I travelled that Fall across the Rockies to take up an appointment teaching English and writing at the University of Calgary.

NFAC has benefited over the years by the involvement of new core faculty and board members not wearied by the decades of struggle since DTUC slipped under the waves. NFAC has found funding for a popular series of artists-in-residence, and hosts a variety of community courses, author readings, theatrical presentations, and artist's exhibitions, residencies and talks. Capacity audiences often attend events in its back-street performance-and-gallery-and-teaching space.

In October 2006, an evening gala was held to celebrate the renaming of NFAC as the Oxygen Art Centre.

Perhaps the new name, like the organization's revitalized spirit, is in keeping with the prediction in Rogers' song. In his lyrics, once the salvagers have sealed the sunken Mary Ellen Carter in preparation to pumping air down to provide the buoyancy necessary to bring the vessel to the surface again, the narrator pauses to announce: "Tomorrow noon, we hit the air and then take up the strain / And watch the Mary Ellen Carter rise again."

Nelson, it seems, will never let NDU, DTUC and now KSA vanish entirely. Like Rogers' sailors, we have "worked like hell to save her, all heedless of the cost." And, like the speaker in the song, we are forever about to succeed.

WHY PROFESS
WHAT IS ABHORRED
The Rescue of Poetry

I

As I was gathering up my papers at the end of class, a young man approached my desk. I was five weeks into teaching a freshman introduction to literature/composition course at a four-year community college in the B.C. Interior. "Well, Tom," the student said. "You did the best you could."

His hand indicated my notes for the four-week-long unit on poetry we had just completed; I had finished the session by assigning the readings for a unit on short stories we would begin the next class. "But I told you the first day," the young man reminded me, "that I came out of high school with definite opinions. Despite your efforts I haven't changed my mind. I still hate poetry."

How can anyone hate poetry? Do they hate sonnets, ballads, villanelles? Rhymed or unrhymed verse? Elizabethan, eighteenth century, Victorian poets? Robert Frost, Robert Lowell, Robert Creeley? Lyric, imagistic, conversational, language-centred techniques? Gwendolyn MacEwan, Susan Musgrave, Erin Mouré? Narrative or non-narrative strategies? Federico Garcia Lorca, Cesar Vallejo, Pablo Neruda? Sound poetry, concrete poetry, prose poetry? Sharon Olds, Carolyn Forché, Rita Dove? Aboriginal, South Asian, revolutionary, feminist, Rasta, work, black, Hispanic, Nuyorican (New York Puerto Rican) poems? Zbigniew Herbert, Tomas Tranströmer, Yehuda Amichai? Those Australian migrants: Thalia, Jeltje, ∏.O.?

The statement *I hate poetry*, which I hear in one form or another whenever I teach an introduction to literature class, is like claiming: "I hate music." Anybody can ferociously dislike Rap or Rachmaninoff, country and western, or John Cage. But I've never heard someone completely dismiss any other form of cultural expression. "I hate abstract art" or even "I hate modern art," okay, sure. But—except referring to a school course and not an area of human endeavour—not: "I hate art."

Nor are creative writing classes exempt. At the start of each postsecondary introductory creative writing class I teach I outline the genres we are going to cover. Inevitably in response I am informed: "Ugh. Not poetry. I hate poetry."

Why does this emotion arise? How is it perpetuated? In my essay "A House Without Books" in my collection *A Country Not Considered: Canada, Culture, Work*, I argue that one important origin for our attitudes to literature is our formal education "since school is the only place most of us ever meet people whose job it is to try to show us the worth of literature" (30). What events occur in elementary, secondary and postsecondary classrooms to cause women and men to decide they detest an entire art form?

In my case, I was blessed with a few teachers who managed to communicate—at least to me—a deep affection for literature. This reinforced the enormous delight in poetry evinced by my father during my childhood. Although my father was a pulp mill chemist, he was passionate about reading, and reading aloud, English poets like A.E. Housman and Alfred Noyes, and Canadian poets like Wilfred Campbell and E. Pauline Johnson. Our house while I was growing up in the 1950s and 1960s also contained well-worn editions of *contemporary* Canadian poets—F.R. Scott, Dorothy Livesay, Earle Birney, Irving Layton, Miriam Waddington. The latest volumes by these and newer writers such as Eli Mandel, Al Purdy, and Leonard Cohen continually arrived.

The enthusiasm that my father and to a lesser extent my mother demonstrated for poetry convinced me that the art mattered, that it had a past, present and a future that held value. Contrasted to these beliefs was the dreary mechanistic attitude to poems taken by some teachers I encountered. In these classrooms, we were directed to closely examine lines for the sole purpose of ascertaining stress patterns and rhyme patterns in order to conclude whether a given fragment of verse—irrespective of meaning or any other artistic consideration—was trochaic or anapestic, whether rhyme schemes were ABBA or ABAB or LSMFT. And even in university, many instructors insisted on one correct interpretation of ambiguous sections or complete poems: such a version was declared right; all other possible readings were decreed null and void. Studying poetry thus was like auto shop or the rifle disassembly/assembly drill in army cadets. Full marks were obtainable if you could name the parts correctly as you took the apparatus apart, and full marks were assigned if you could follow the approved method of reattaching the pieces back into working order as speedily as possible. The poetry portion of English *exams*, which frequently asked you to discuss a poem you had never seen before, resembled the army exercise whereby cadets were required to break down and reassemble a rifle *blindfolded*. The only difference was that a reassembled poem could not fire a bullet. The poem instead squatted inertly on its white page, blanketed metaphorically with comments superimposed on it in red pencil: a distorted, hideous thing.

My discussions with my students over the years has led me to conclude that for the majority of them my worst experiences match their recent interactions with poetry in institutions of learning. During early adolescence these young men and women often sought to express their feelings about their emerging selves in a free-form style of writing they called poetry. At various times the lyrics of certain popular songs, the words emotionally bolstered by effects generated by the accompanying music, speak to them with unusual force or meaning. But such encounters that suggest the incipient power of words presented in a non-prose format are light-years distant from the way poetry was inflicted on them in school.

Exposure to poetry was used as a measure on the basis of which the student was pronounced stupid, unimaginative, a failure. Who would not hate an activity or artifact that authority utilizes to brand us with these labels? Formal schooling in many subjects frequently diminishes a student's self-respect in this manner. Mathematics, history, science classes can be taught so as to primarily instruct us that we are brainless, lazy, worthless. Yet at least in these subjects the teacher can indicate how our shortcomings in these fields will have direct and dire consequences in adult life: these areas of instruction are clearly necessary to succeed on many jobs, or to comprehend what is happening in the world in which we are supposed to be citizens. But poetry? Why are we made to feel badly about ourselves over a subject which no instructor bothers to even *try* to claim has the slightest use outside of school? We can grudgingly admit that we cannot escape the influence on our lives of biology, physics, geography—regardless of how badly taught, and of how our reaction to that pedagogy may have damaged our self-esteem. Even our shortcomings in English classes other than those associated with poetry—spelling, or crafting a lucid, grammatically correct sentence—we can acknowledge could affect us negatively after we have graduated or dropped out of school. One way or another our inabilities in these areas might surface to impair our functioning as adults. But if there is one subject in which we were pronounced incompetent on which we can *afford* afterwards to vent our anger and dismay at how school labelled us, that subject is poetry. Given its lack of status or relevance in the larger world, poetry is the perfect receptacle for our rage and frustration. Like any powerless minority, poetry is safe to despise, loathe, abhor.

As a poet, I am not happy with the current situation. Can poetry be taught so that it is not detested, not asked to bear the sins of mass public education? After all, a hatred of poetry does not even restore the self-respect of the despiser. Rather, this abhorrence when expressed serves as a restatement or reminder of the perceived inadequacies of the person uttering the emotion. So this venting reinforces the pattern that equates the art form with a poor self-image. And the expression of this dislike obviously does poetry no good. We need to stop the cycle of hate for the sake both of the victims of certain pedagogical practices and of the art itself.

I believe effective change proceeds from understanding root causes of inappropriate or destructive behaviour. We have to ask, then, two questions. The first is: what do we teach poetry *for*? That is, what is our aim in including poetry as part of the English curriculum at any level? The second question is: what do we teach *poetry* for? In an era when poetry is a thoroughly marginalized art form, what positive contribution can a poem make to human existence? Whatever poetry's usefulness to society might have been in the past, why seek to encompass the art now in our educational system? Why not recognize that poetry is a superseded group of artistic strategies? My two main questions here are obviously interrelated, although I will consider them in sequence.

II

First, when I walk into a classroom to instruct people about poetry, what should my intention be? I believe my achievement as an instructor must be judged by whether those who experience my pedagogy leave the class with a love of the art. According to this standard, the student I refer to at the start of this article represents a failure on my part. Ideally, any material I introduce to my students, including any artistic technique I draw to their attention or expect them to become proficient in understanding and describing, will contribute to initiating or affirming an *affection* on their part toward poetry.

I want the students to emerge from the class as enlightened amateur readers of poetry: amateur, where the word means "lover of." Educational administrators and others are often startled when I insist that even when we teach creative writing, our fundamental goal is to produce careful, knowledgeable *readers* rather than professional writers. Upwards of 98 per cent of those we teach in English or writing classes will never become professional critics of poetry or become poets. This outcome is identical to how very few students in the fine arts will continue on to become professional painters or sculptors, and few people who take guitar lessons will become professional rock or classical guitarists. The foremost pedagogical objective of our poetry classes consequently must be to produce an interested and informed *audience* for poetry.

The foundation of any curriculum in poetry should be to provide students with a wide exposure to examples of the art—whatever the historical era or theme or other focus of the course. Students then need to be encouraged, in as open an atmosphere as possible, to articulate and defend their responses to these poems. This goal requires that the student have the tools with which to examine their own reaction to a poem. Students also need the tools to successfully communicate that response to others. The student has to be able to show—not just tell—others why she or he responds as she or he does to a poem (and thus defend her or his reaction). These same analytic skills allow a student to thoroughly absorb lessons gathered from her or his reading, or from hearing the comments of classmates or the instructor about such poems. The student can then more knowledgeably reject, accept or adapt this input, fine-tuning her or his appreciation of the art.

A poetry curriculum therefore must involve a safe, supportive, and informed environment in which students can critique the writing of contemporary or historical authors as well as the response of other class members to these poems. Students need to practice the skills necessary to effectively formulate, support and communicate their judgments of writing to which they are introduced. By so doing, a student exercises and refines skills in critical (in both senses) thinking, writing and reading.

At the very least, a course in poetry should not leave students with a dislike—or increased dislike—of the art form. What conceivable use can such a pedagogical outcome be? Yet at present this is the curriculum's net effect on many, if not most, students. How does this result help the student? Help the art form? Help the arts or humanities or the community or any larger reality or abstraction? To me, a course of studies in poetry instead should improve the student's ability to recognize and enjoy the subtleties as well as the more evident achievements of the art. A student should discover or further augment within himself or herself an awareness of the power of the written word to communicate and initiate ideas and emotions. The result of the course's accomplishments should be a feeling of pleasurable wonder at what the human race, via this art form—via *words*—has wrought.

I believe that the negative reaction to poetry created by pedagogies employed today often arises from a different, unstated curriculum objective: to develop professional critics. My teaching experience convinces me that unless students understand why this or that critical method enhances their delight in an art form, the application of any critical theory becomes for most students an exercise in drudgery, in irrelevant make-work. Inculcating and/or preserving a love of poetry must be the intent of any application of a specific critical approach to the art. One important danger in proceeding otherwise is that as each new generation of teachers at any level is trained, these men and women are trained to dislike or despise poetry.

I have certainly witnessed firsthand the consequence of the existing pedagogy not only as a student but as an instructor. When certain disciplines in many B.C. Interior colleges expanded in the early 1990s by government fiat from two-year to four-year programs, some institutions suffered the inflow of new English PhDs produced in graduate seminars that appeared to have been steeped in either vicious competitiveness or competitive viciousness. Far from producing teachers with a love of the art or the artists in their chosen field, these graduate schools unleashed new instructors who behaved very much like abused children. Smarting from some series of crushing blows to their self-esteem, the new professors sought to vent their anger on any target they deemed powerless—from their hapless students to any colleague they concluded was vulnerable to some form of academic scorn or punishment. Supersaturated themselves with the jargon of the critical stance favoured at their alma mater—a jargon which will date the would-be scholars more rapidly than they imagine—these instructors attempted to drench any and all within their academic reach with a language comprehensible only to a highly specialized few.

The effect of such behaviour on anyone's appreciation of the art form they supposedly profess was never a factor for these instructors' consideration. I can recall one newly-minted colleague spluttering in opposition to a curriculum proposal, opining that the suggested approach was wrong because it "would privilege the writer over the critic."

Such extreme outcomes of an unhelpful graduate pedagogy are a continuation of long-standing trends in the teaching of literature, however. In an essay, "The Enemies of Intelligence," published in my 1983 *Inside Job: Essays on the New Work Writing*, I trace the consequences for the literary arts of how the formerly touted *mythic* criticism was adopted into teaching procedures:

> [M]ythic criticism, like any critical school based on material remote from most people's daily experiences, inevitably produces a jargon unfamiliar to ordinary citizens. Thus, if someone wishes to become a professional literary scholar, he or she must be taught a new language as well as the approved ways of considering literature. In practice, this process of training literary academics incorporates many of the same techniques used in basic training of army inductees: an instilling of the habit of obedience in the trainee by the assignment of meaningless and time-consuming tasks; forced acceptance by the trainee of the world view of the trainer through a system of rewards and punishments; and the removal of the trainee from the usual civilian frames of reference, including common sense.
>
> The results of an educational process so distanced from the concerns of everyday life are poor. The trivial nature of much literary research is already a byword among people with any sort of perspective on the literary scholar's occupation. The failure of university English classes to generate enthusiasm for either the classics of our literature or

for contemporary imaginative writing is evidenced in the reading habits of a majority of the population—both those who attended these classes themselves and those who were instructed in school by those who attended these classes. The lack of command of English spelling, grammar and composition on the part of university graduates is an old complaint, but at best the situation is not improving.

In addition, the current training and practice of most literary scholars ensures that contemporary criticism, like contemporary literature, will not develop into an opportunity for accurate critical reflection on society but remains an elaborate game with esoteric rules. … [S]tudents are mainly bored or flabbergasted by this procedure, but here and there a student will resolve to devote himself or herself to mastering this "professional" behaviour. And so the pattern is reproduced again. What could be a chance for students to acquire skills necessary for an intelligent and creative assessment of what words can do—not just in literature but also in advertising, politics and other experiences of everyday existence—instead becomes a means by which students learn that a work of literature is a puzzle which is difficult and probably pointless to try to solve. (86-88)

Central to transforming the usual effect of our present pedagogical approach to poetry is to familiarize students with the broadest possible scope of the art. As I note above, this is the foundation of a syllabus whose goal is to achieve and sustain a love for poetry. Regardless of how a course is organized—historically, thematically, or concentrating on technique—the aim here is to ensure a student does not conclude poetry inhabits only a narrow band of the art's actual spectrum. The more expansive the student's exposure to poetry is, the more likely the work of some poet will engage the sensibilities of the student.

Of the various kinds of music I hear, how little engages me, strongly moves me. If I listened to just a few styles, eras, themes, or musicians, I might decide there is not much to interest me about music. The women's movement, the new self-consciousness of various minorities, the increased attention to literary translation all have helped make available poetries supplementary to the established canon. A revelation of the full literary context—historical or modern—in which a poet plied her or his art also helps illustrate for the student poetry's immense range.

This need to impress upon students the multifariousness of poetry is subverted, however, by the standard teaching anthology. With rare exceptions, teaching anthologies are generated from existing anthologies rather than from primary source research. As a result, the same set pieces tend to appear over and over. This selection process shrinks poetry to a smaller presence than that required to improve the current circumstances of the art. Anthology editors would claim they are distilling the essence of poetry; I would propose that in some cases they are desiccating poetry. The endlessly-taught "important" poems can become the clichés of the art. And the original power of the poet's expression wears extremely thin after someone has presented the piece without enthusiasm or insight too many times in classroom after classroom.

I feel that most teaching anthologies, despite the artistic achievement of their contents, represent the same sort of pit or black hole for poetry that the big annual folk music festivals like Vancouver's do for the real world of folk song. Attending such a festival can be a pleasant occurrence: I am introduced to high calibre music previously unknown to me, and if I'm lucky, I get to hear some old favourites. But attending the festival, for most men and women in the audience, is an experience that extracts from them virtually all the time, effort and money they are ever going to expend responding to the art form. Ongoing folk music activities in people's own communities largely remains hidden from them, eclipsed by the glitter of the lavish, institutionalized event. Community money (from every tier of government) and publicity that might succour a lively resident folk music tradition are mostly siphoned into the festival. The potential audience for a broader range of folk music, performed throughout the year in a wider variety of venues, is lost to a one-time-only crowd. Local folk club members will argue that the health of their art is harmed, not helped, by the disproportionate attention showered on one selection of their art.

Finding alternatives or supplements to a teaching anthology of course involves skill and ingenuity. Technically, the photocopier is an instructor's chief ally in the rescue of poetry, despite the threat of Canada's misguided copyright provisions. Also, where the syllabus permits, assigning as a text an entire book by a local writer, or by an author who will be reading in the community or school during the semester, is another means to boost students' awareness of poetry's rich texture and extent.

Discovering *what* to photocopy or assign remains a vital task for teachers wishing to adopt new materials. Obviously if an instructor hates poetry herself or himself, such a professional development chore will be regarded with distaste. As well, if a teacher fundamentally dis-likes poetry, or has been persuaded by his or her own wretched expe-riences in school that she or he is unable to discern value in any poem not previously approved by others, such a teacher is unlikely to choose material that will effectively inspire delight or affection in students.

For those with enough self-confidence in their enjoyment of the art to seek fresh poems, at the moment only a wide reading with an open mind can provide pedagogically useful examples of writing. I would like to see a more formal expansion of the informal sharing of teach-able poems that exists among poetry-friendly colleagues who already know each other. Some form of mandatory continuing education in the pedagogy of literature could serve in a more organized way to provide teachers at all levels with a source of poetries that work well in the classroom to ignite a love of the art in students. This requirement might reinforce the concept that instructors need to expand their pedagogical repertoire throughout their careers in order to continually improve their teaching. Or maybe such upgrading should be manda-tory only in subject areas where present teaching styles and syllabuses produce demonstrably negative results, as with poetry!

III

Yet, whatever our pedagogical goal, why bother teaching poetry at all? Given that time is at a premium in our educational process, why is poetry a fit subject when the art's current marginal status is attested to by various measurable standards? For instance, small press publishers have complained to me that whereas thirty or forty years ago a new collection of poems by a Canadian author routinely sold a pitiful 1,200 copies, a similar book these days is lucky to sell 500. And this despite a surge in the size of the population, and decades of phenomenal growth in postsecondary institutions—each of which offers literature courses as a requirement. To the mystification and shame of my colleagues who teach creative writing, during this same period the number of graduates from our programs in imaginative writing has also escalated, without affecting these sad statistics. Even in the U.S., if books by contemporary poets sell more readily than the norm for poetry, the authors almost invariably are known to the public for having achieved celebrity in other fields: as novelists (Margaret Atwood, for example), or as musicians (Leonard Cohen, for example) or as incarnations of cultural postures or concepts (Sylvia Plath as tormented genius/woman-as-victim, or Robert Bly as a founder of the men's movement).

One societal trend in the new millennium is for us more frequently to be spectators of, instead of participants in, our lives—to be listeners to music, for instance, rather than singers or performers ourselves. In accordance with this development, I encounter less and less frequently people who enjoy the memorization and recitation of poems. The generation that delighted in knowing by heart Robert Burns or Robert W. Service is vanishing, and is not being replaced. Nor is verse by other poets committed to memory by the extensive cross section of people as once could recite work by a variety of bards.

Where attraction to types of poetry among a larger population has recently surfaced—for instance, cowboy poetry, or spoken word poetry, or Rap with its insistent rhyming couplets—the appeal of these forms of the art mainly lie elsewhere than in use of language. The basis for the more widespread response to these manifestations of poetry is primarily theatrical spectacle—consumption of a public performance. With rare exceptions, these versions of the art do not repay close reading; whenever the verse is considered outside of the spectacle (or in the case of popular music, when separated from the musical accompaniment), the words' emotional power weakens noticeably or disappears. Books by these poetry performance artists do not sell in significant numbers. This is not art one takes home, or to heart, in written form.

The Internet is sometimes lauded as the locale of a renaissance of interest in publishing poetry. As nearly as I can ascertain, though, the establishment of electronic magazines and the enormous opportunity for self-publishing available online remains a matter of "give" rather than "get." Staring into a monitor screen is a notoriously stressful way to receive information of any kind. I have never experienced and cannot imagine reading for pleasure from such a source. Use of e-book readers, now that their novelty is wearing off, increasingly seems limited to travellers. Although I am in close contact with a number of fellow writers, teaching colleagues and students who are 'Net aficionados, I have never yet heard a single one recommend enthusiastically a *poem* they discovered online. These 'Net surfers frequently are excited and fascinated by *information* they glean among the electrons. The literature posted at so many sites, though, seems to be scanned simply as information, as the 'Net users characteristically skip over the unscrolling acres of words and images in search of a jolt, a charge, some astonishment or other frisson.

Body hunched forward, face inches from a screen, is not a posture conducive to a leisurely and careful reading of a literary text. The Internet may well serve as the depository for poems which formerly the lonely and socially inept consigned to their desk drawer. But of all the literary arts, poetry least rewards the act of browsing through words, and browsing (a.k.a. surfing) is the quintessential human interaction online. Downloading writing, printing it off, and then attempting to read it offers more benign possibilities. But a sheaf of printer paper is in effect an unbound book: a loose collection of sheets not conducive to portability or ease of perusal.

So if poetry today is firmly marginalized, why involve it in our curriculums? My answer originates with the expression of wonder and joy I encounter each term when a student truly connects with a poem. "Wow," the student will effuse, "I didn't know a poem could be about this." Or: "This poem really touched me in a way I haven't felt before." A power exists in these words that completes an emotional circuit between author and reader.

Certain assemblages of words we call poems succeed beyond question at bridging the essential solitude of human existence. Each of us is alive in a fleshly and perishable body, linked however tenuously to family and community, to a social past and present. Despite our connections with others, each of us labours basically alone to experience and process our life. What *relief*—for surely that is at the root of the exhilaration we feel when a work of art overwhelms us—to sense that another human voice possesses the ability to stir us, to reach our emotional and/or intellectual core: to reassure us that our feelings and thoughts are shared, or to expose us to emotions, ideas, and perspectives not previously encountered.

Meaningful art is a profound act of solidarity: a declaration, via the artist's communication of her or his vision to me, of my participation in the human story. My acknowledgement of a specific poem's efficacy at engaging me validates the poet's imagination and artistic toil. Simultaneously, due to the literary artifact's successful transfer of an emotional or intellectual stimulation from the author to me, I have enriched my life. As long as a poem is able to enhance a man's or woman's perception of what it means to be human, the art form proves its worth. Each time I observe the face of a student shine with a radiance not evident before a poem was read, absorbed, agreed with, my faith in the value of poetry and the teaching of poetry is confirmed.

The very definition of the art, though, poses problems as well as reasons for instruction in it. I consider poetry to be the most intense possible use of language. Traditional poems employ regular patterns of stress, sound and/or stanza in order to create linguistic intenseness, to call attention to the difference between what the poem wishes to communicate and everyday speech. But the very regularity of these patterns infers predictability, and predictability can lessen the reader's attention, can detract from intensity.

Regular patterns were largely abandoned by poets early in the twentieth century. Belief in established arrangements and hierarchies in social, religious, scientific and artistic life was crumbling around the poets. And any concept of predictable orderliness in these spheres continued to be challenged as the century proceeded. The employment of regular patterns as a compositional strategy seemed an ineffective way to depict life in an era of uncertainties.

Yet when poets discard regular templates for metre, rhyme and stanza, the problem of creating intensity increases. How can poets draw attention to the difference between their discourse and everyday speech without resorting to predictable patterns? Language somehow must work harder than with conventional prose—or else why call what is written a poem? Moreover, the reader's passage through the words must be slowed down enough that he or she becomes aware of the way language is functioning more adroitly than it does in prose.

Since the methods of creating intensity have to be unpredictable, however, a second problem arises. Readers are asked to enter unfamiliar ground each time they are invited to read a non-traditional poem. In effect, the poet invents the art form every time he or she writes, and this fact may enormously discomfit the intended audience. Similar to the uncertainty experienced whenever someone encounters the unexpected in any genre of contemporary art, how can a reader be sure the writing he or she is faced with has merit?

The strategies chosen to alert the reader that she or he must read the poem differently than prose can include playful, fractured and/or ambiguous use of sense, grammar, spelling, sound. The page can serve as a canvas: indents, typography, and stanza and line breaks may impart meaning visually. Use of metaphors, similes, hyperbole or images that draw on esoteric knowledge are other compositional devices contemporary poets may adopt.

Meanwhile, the more extreme nature of some attempts to distinguish poetry from conventional prose can alienate readers if the *purpose* of adopting a particular compositional technique is not understood, or is deliberately mystified in a defensive gesture on the part of the writer. When poetry is already disliked by the population for reasons discussed above, and then poetry is further cloaked in an aura of difficult access, the combination can only be bad news for the art. The B.C. poet and publisher Howard White describes an Amnesty International-sponsored encounter between Canadian and foreign writers in Toronto:

> At a bull session later some CanLit prof asked why poetry was less marginalized in so many developing countries and about 17 third-worlders tried to answer at once. The general drift was, western poets have done it to themselves because all they do is write for each other. They consider it corruption of true art to write for common taste, but they're never done whining that the public fails to appreciate them. And even when poets from developing countries show how well the public responds to poets who write for common taste with serious purpose, western writers fail to get the message. Somebody tried to make a case that western writers didn't have the kind of big social challenges poets in developing worlds did, but gave up when somebody else yelled, "Try taking your culture back from Hollywood and Madison Avenue!" (10-11)

A variety of approaches to creating an intense use of language is *bound* to produce artistic disagreements, though. Intensity, after all, is not a quality capable of objective measurement. The Chilean poet Nicanor Parra cautions against claims that one specific technique will be the salvation of poetry, or that any such strategy is the only correct one for whatever reason. His poem "Young Poets" is here translated by Miller Williams:

Write as you will
In whatever style you like
Too much blood has run under the bridge
To go on believing
That only one road is right.

In poetry everything is permitted.

With only this condition, of course:
You have to improve on the blank page. (143)

I regard the uncertainty swirling around the corpus of contemporary poetry—and, by extension, historical poetries—as a marvellous and unique opportunity for learning. This situation constitutes for me a further justification of poetry's inclusion in our schools. Poetry raises an abundance of questions about linguistic expression, about the purpose and function of art, about the formation of personal judgment, about the skills necessary to form and defend in words an opinion or idea. Revealing the craft of poetry can initiate students into the craft of other artistic media—music, cinema, clay, fibre arts. What are the technical means these arts employ to generate their range of effects on people? Issues of marginality and the mainstream, of the role of cultural gatekeepers, of speech and silence are inherent in any study of poetry. Where students are shown poems that successfully enlarge their sense of the world, of the myriad possibilities of human life, of other ways of envisioning the challenge of being human, the art has unquestionably earned its place in any curriculum designed to educate minds rather than merely train them.

Indeed, an inquiry into the very basis of much of the educational process—labelling, categorizing—is subsumed by an examination of poetry. How can there be both prose poems and poetic prose? In the latter case, if poetry is writing at its most intense, can the "small dream about time" (140) in Annie Dillard's non-fiction *Pilgrim at Tinker Creek*—the riveting sequence where the book's narrator views all the temporal content of the Earth at a single glance (140-143)—not be called poetry? Or what about the evocative image that closes Sid

Marty's non-fiction *Men for the Mountains*, where the novice national park employee listens to the shade of legendary Jasper Park warden George Busby?

> He leaned forward then and held his gnarled hands out to the firelight, and the flames threw his shadow, magnified, onto the thick logs of the cabin wall. Then he began to weave a tale of high mountains and of proud men that rode among them, like princes surveying their estates, like lords high up in their strongholds, where only the wind could touch them, and where the world was free of pain and sorrow, and we were always young. (270)

If such prose words can be termed poetry, what is the purpose of nomenclature? What does it mean to exist at a time when boundaries between the various arts are collapsing, when even some sciences are apparently converging?

In our culture at present, the most widely accepted means of determining value is cash: anything that cannot attract dollars is judged worthless. Yet poetry exists entirely outside the money economy. Almost no book of poetry makes a profit; virtually no poets can live on sales of their art. To continue to honour poetry—to deem the art culturally significant—is to instruct students that some things on this planet have value even if those things cannot be assigned a monetary equivalent. Few people would attend a church that lacked a building, that was so poor the congregation met in the open air. Few sports or games—even among children—are now played without prior purchase of expensive equipment. But poetry insists that there *is* a worth beyond dollars, that some human activities and creations are literally priceless.

Not that poetry lacks a defense even in terms of its usefulness to commerce, to the pursuit of money. For instance communications consultant Cheryl Reimold, in a four-part series published in the magazine of the U.S. Technical Association of the Pulp and Paper Industry, explains why reading poetry would be helpful to business people. She introduces her first article by suggesting:

> To your regular diet of technical or business material, add
> a little poetry. Wait, please—don't stop reading this yet!
> I'm not suggesting this only to offer you the aesthetic and
> spiritual gifts of poetry. Poetry will help you write better
> memos, letters, and reports.
> Great poetry releases the power in ordinary words and
> makes them resonate. The poets take all the principles of
> writing—persuasion, clarity, organization, force—and
> exploit them to the maximum. In a few words, they can
> tell the story of the world. To discover the possibilities in
> language and use it to transmit your message with real clar-
> ity and power—you must read poetry. (97)

I locate poetry's merit as a subject for study at considerable remove
from Reimold's claim that exposure to some poems will spice up a
corporate executive's memos. But I certainly endorse her praise for
the best poets: "In a few words, they can tell the story of the world."
Whatever small amount most of us know about the Elizabethans or
Victorians, we know from poems that have lasted. The mighty armies,
fleets, battles, social unrest have faded with the kings, the queens,
the wealthy, the successful entrepreneurs, the desperately poor. Some
words were scratched on paper by one particular human, on a Thurs-
day afternoon when a rainstorm seemed imminent and a couple of
domestic responsibilities—involving a rip in a coat and a diminished
household fuel supply—were being evaded. Improbably, those words
are what has endured. The noisy among us today are certain that the
sense of our own era we will bequeath to the generations to come will
involve movies, television, the latest pop music star. Perhaps. But so
far among humanity's achievements, poems have proven among the
most effective messengers from the past to the future.

I believe that when we teach our students affection for poetry, we
teach them affection for the human story as it has been, as it is, and as
it will be. Which is to say that as we rescue poetry for love, we teach our
students love for their own species, and so themselves. Surely that deserves
our best efforts as teachers; surely our profession has no more crucial task.

WORKS CITED

Dillard, Annie. *Pilgrim at Tinker Creek*. New York: HarperCollins, 1988. Print.

Marty, Sid. *Men For the Mountains*. Toronto: McClelland and Stewart, 1978. Print.

Parra, Nicanor. *Poems and Antipoems*. New York: New Directions, 1966. Print.

Reimold, Cheryl. "Principles from Poetry. Part 1: Persuasion." *Tappi Journal* 68.12 (1985): 97. Print.

Wayman, Tom. *A Country Not Considered: Canada, Culture, Work*. Concord, ON: Anansi, 1993. Print.

—. *Inside Job: Essays on the New Work Writing*. Madeira Park, B.C.: Harbour, 1983. Print.

White, Howard. *Ghost in the Gears*. Madeira Park, B.C.: Harbour, 1993. Print.

PADDLING TOWARD
A BETTER WORLD
On George Hitchcock (1914-2010)
and *Kayak* (1964-1984)

As a writing MFA student at the University of California at Irvine 1966-68, I was impressed by the San Francisco (later Santa Cruz) literary magazine, *Kayak*, edited by George Hitchcock. I regarded *Kayak*'s chief paddler as a role model, though I never met the man. The two blades on his paddle that I admired from afar were generosity and activism. A third aspect to George Hitchcock I wanted to emulate was the varnish coating both blades: a sense of humour.

Though *Kayak*'s standards were high, Mr. Hitchcock was always generous in his brief comments rejecting my poems and those of my friends from the UCI graduate program. His penned responses to our work were unfailingly encouraging, albeit often specific about what he saw in our work that was not as strong as it could be. At the same time, the odd and funny illustrations on the rejections were cheering, and reminded us not to take this process of submission and rejection too seriously. Even the magazine's masthead comment, which reminded the reader that a kayak has never been a vehicle for mass transit, spoke metaphorically about how a poem that one person considers a work of poetic genius, capable of transporting that person into ecstasies, is to another person incomprehensible twaddle. The metaphor was simultaneously funny, astute, and a provider of much-needed perspective to me as a young writer.

Mr. Hitchcock's generosity was as much active as passive, though: he found space aboard *Kayak* for our best efforts. That is, spurred on by our enjoyment of the magazine's content, and inspired by the way his jotted comments when rejecting us never foreclosed the possibility of future acceptance, we were encouraged to draw from deeper down in our writing and revising. Eventually, he published poems of ours, to our enormous delight. The jovial if exacting spirit of the craft's skipper that came through every aspect of the magazine added a human touch to the—let's face it—humiliating process of being rejected over and over. An acceptance from *Kayak* felt like you had achieved a chance to participate in a unique project: a different feeling from that provided by an acceptance from slicker, more austere magazines. Placing a poem with the latter were mere accomplishments, notches on an imaginary stick that you hoped one day to wave before potential publishers of a first book. But having your words appear in *Kayak* was an event: you felt you had joined a family you were pleased be part of, or an expedition you wanted to travel with, or had been accepted into a club of which, unlike Groucho, you were proud to be a member.

Besides, or maybe integral with, that generous welcoming spirit, was Mr. Hitchcock's activism: his evident belief that poetry and revolutionary socialism were inseparable. After all, the surrealism that frequently was found among *Kayak*'s cargo was born out of the conviction that changing old perceptions of the world would lead humanity to construct via revolution a more just, more equitable society. "Surrealism: the communism of genius?" the Parisian Surrealist Central asked in the 1920s. The question was open-ended, but more declarative was another slogan of the Parisian group: "If you love love, you will love surrealism." The Argentinian fighter in the Cuban revolt against the dictator Fulgencio Batista, Che Guevara, had pronounced that a true revolutionary is guided by great feelings of love. When, as a wounded and helpless captured guerrilla in another struggle against a Latin American oligarch, Guevara was murdered in 1967 in Bolivia, *Kayak* sponsored an elegy contest for him. I cannot emphasize enough that in the context of the time this was a daring move for a U.S. literary magazine. Guevara was still regarded widely as a godless Communist menace to U.S. control of the hemisphere; his image had not yet been turned into a brand adorning dozens of consumer trinkets as a vague symbol of teen angst.

The elegy contest created quite a stir. And I don't think Mr. Hitchcock, with his abiding sense of humour, of perspective, would have objected to the complaint of the poet J.D. Whitney in what for me was the best 1960s poetry anthology, *The Whites of Their Eyes*, edited by Seattle's Paul Hunter, and Patti and Tom Parson (Seattle: Consumption, 1970). Whitney in his poem "Che" notes that elegies are to some degree evasion

> unless
> > we took a thousand elegies
> chiseled on a huge
> > > stone fist
> and shoved it
> > up the asshole of
> imperialism
>
> now
> > that would
> be some tribute

Kayak itself makes an appearance in *The Whites of Their Eyes*, incidentally, in that a poem by Charles Simic from his 1967 collection *What the Grass Says,* published by Kayak books, made the cut.

Of course, the melding of poetry with the tangible struggle for a fairer, more liveable world was evident many places in *Kayak*'s heyday, since poetry was part of publications and rallies connected to the civil rights, anti-Vietnam War, anti-draft, anti-imperialist, Black Power and women's movements. But I can't think of a purely "literary" publication other than *Kayak* that encouraged its contributors to mourn the loss of a revolutionary socialist leader.

My students today find alien the concepts that poetry should have a part in the muck and sweat of the real-world struggle for a better life for all, and that poetry should subsume both generosity and a perspective-granting sense of humour. Many of my writing students have adopted instead the fantasy paradigm that, because they have received much attention in the tiny poetry world on their campuses, they will quickly ascend to a stellar, lucrative career in poetry in the larger world. Poetry is a kind of grease that will lubricate their heady slide upwards, simultaneously defying gravity, the odds, and common sense. They find this world-view reinforced when reading organizers introduce poets by reeling off the awards and prizes and other honours these writers have garnered, saying not a word about any *poems* the authors have written that live in the hearts or minds of anyone.

But there's a brittle kind of energy around the careerist hustling that accompanies the attempt to live out that paradigm. It is an approach to art that divides art's practitioners into winners and losers. While my students are convinced they are winners, my sense is that at the first real artistic setback they face, many of them will feel like losers to themselves and abandon their art entirely.

Robert Bly once distinguished between a poetry *community*—which contains, speaks to, and hears from people of every sort from every walk of life, as irritating as that can be sometimes—and a poetry *network*— which is usually an academic or artistic specialist talking to another academic or artistic specialist. A community, Bly pointed out, will sustain you through good times and bad, whereas a network is strictly an aid to social mobility. If you falter or stray in your pursuit of the network's approved version of success, you are cast aside and nobody cares. For the long run, community is your best bet.

My students don't believe in this distinction. Obviously I and my peers who share a different point of view than our students have not been as successful at showing the alternative as Mr. Hitchcock was. He gave us good advice by example, advice that has sustained us and made our lives (and poetry, I like to think) better than it would otherwise have been. I can pass along this approach to poetry here, likely preaching to the converted. But by and large I have failed to convincingly convey these ideas in the seminar room, where such advice perhaps matters more.

AVANT-GARDE OR LOST PLATOON?
Postmodernism as Social Control

I

Imagine the worries of a conservative North American university or college professor in June 1970. To him or her, the attitudes, beliefs and behaviour of some young people generally and students particularly during the past few years threatens not just the rational operation of a postsecondary institution—negatively impacting the classroom as well as institutional goals and decision-making structures. In addition, off-campus protest activities by young men and women—demonstrations, sit-ins, boycotts—plus the personal appearance and declared viewpoints of a segment of youth indicate an apparent wish by an ever-growing minority to reject all social norms, including legitimate efforts to contain Communism's spread at home and abroad, and attempts by legally constituted authorities to oversee the participation of North America's coloured population in their country's economic and social mainstreams.

On campus, this oppositional spirit of some students would seem to our professor to have a disruptive effect far beyond their numbers. Impudent in-class questions with regard to the "relevance" of course content, so-called "teach-ins" regarding social issues such as the Vietnam War or civil rights for Negroes, and production of institutional "anti-calendars" which unfairly and ignorantly critique both individual professors' teaching abilities and the courses themselves are just a few of the ways the normal functioning of the institution has been hampered or endangered. Protest rallies held on campus to object to this or that policy of the school's administration, or of democratically elected or appointed off-campus authority at every level, plus the selling or free distribution on campus of agitational left-wing propaganda in the form of leaflets, pamphlets and "underground newspapers," also have sought to undermine postsecondary education's true purpose: the pursuit of knowledge useful for the orderly enhancement of a democratic society, and the mental and moral shaping of those young men and women who someday will guide private and public enterprises, not to mention the nation itself, into the future.

Most upsetting in the eyes of our professor is that the disruptive ideas and activities of a small number of students—ironically, many of whom are ostensibly studying disciplines considered part of the "humanities"—has led to a complete shut-down of a campus, as at Columbia University in the spring of 1968 and San Francisco State College that fall. Even Harvard suffered through a student "strike" in April of 1969. And repeatedly campus buildings in many institutions have been temporarily "occupied" by bands of students, who thus deny access to classrooms, laboratories, and faculty or administrative offices to those who legitimately have a right to use them. Such building take-overs—for purposes of general protest, and to prevent military and corporate recruiting—swelled to 313 in the U.S. during the 1969-70 academic year, according to the FBI. A survey of only a tenth of America's 2,000 campuses showed that in the first six months of 1969 more than 200,000 students were involved in protests, with 3,600 of them arrested and nearly 1,000 suspended or expelled (Hayden 393). And so far in 1970 the numbers appear higher.

Our professor is aware that, given the nature of many on-campus protest activities, radical students regard as porous the boundary between an academic institution and the surrounding society. So the danger seems real and immediate that the half-baked ideas of some students might find resonance among disgruntled youth not currently enjoying the privilege of attending a university or college. The May 1968 events in Paris, which saw students and young union militants bring much of the city to a standstill, represent an example of what might yet occur in North America. One group of student activists visible on U.S. campuses is already calling for a "worker-student alliance," while in Detroit some Negro auto-plant workers formed a Dodge Revolutionary Union Movement in spring 1968. An illegal strike of theirs even involved participation by white employees. By last June several such groups of Negro car-factory employees had established a League of Revolutionary Black Workers (Ahmad).

How far this potential insurrectionary contamination of the off-campus world by misguided young people could go is indicated by a group advocating outright terrorism that broke away the previous June from the largest U.S. radical student organization, the Students for a Democratic Society. The breakaway faction, calling itself the Weathermen, managed to kill three of their own this March when a bomb factory in a Greenwich Village townhouse exploded. And in early June a police headquarters in New York was bombed by the group, although no one was hurt.

To our professor, the authorities' counter to date to the burgeoning student and youth unrest represents no solution. Instead of mounting a civilized, vigorous and persuasive intellectual defense of the status quo, or adopting some other morally and scholarly sound initiative to restore the campuses to sanity, the powers-that-be appear to have adopted a Third-World-type escalation of deadly violence. In April this year, a student was shot and killed by police during protest riots in the Isla Vista student district alongside the University of California at Santa Barbara campus. Then in early May, in response to the U.S. invasion on April 30 of Cambodia, announced as necessary to defeat the Communist insurgents in Vietnam, four students peacefully participating in an anti-invasion demonstration at Kent State University in Ohio were gunned down by National Guardsmen, and a further eleven wounded. These shootings prompted a week of nationwide protest, with more than 300 university and college campuses closed either in response to demonstrations or pre-emptively. Ten days after the Kent State incident, two student protesters were killed and nine wounded by police gunfire on the Jackson State University campus in Mississippi.

When our professor reviews the current crisis facing universities and colleges, he or she rejects as extreme the option of quieting postsecondary institutions by killing any young person who advocates unpopular ideas in a peaceful manner. Instead, our professor dreams of introducing into scholarly pursuits, especially those in the humanities and social science disciplines from which the majority of student protestors have come, a new and different slate of concepts whose embrace by students would result in calming the campus, and hence the surrounding society, where young people have been riled up by agitation originating in postsecondary institutions.

To be effective at pacifying the campus, the professor realizes, the alternative set of ideas would have to simultaneously:

- Convince students that nothing is "true." Activism begins with a conviction that certain ideas, facts or actions are right, and others are wrong. Undermine this conviction and you undermine the motivation for protest: no one is going to march in the street or otherwise demand changes on behalf of a concept that he or she feels perhaps is not true.
- Undermine the ability of students to speak clearly to the off-campus population about the social, political or economic situation. People with a postsecondary education are, after all, an elite, and like any elite should demonstrate this status by employment of a jargon—a kind of insider's shorthand or shop-talk—as well as references to esoteric knowledge not possessed by the hoi polloi. This component of the new set of concepts can build on some activists' present use in speeches and writing of Maoist and

other revolutionary terminology unfamiliar (and baffling, not to mention off-putting) to a non-specialist audience.

- Counter the sense of solidarity on which any mass movement depends by encouraging students to focus on the needs and wishes of particular societal groups. By encouraging students to narrow their attention to any specific splinter identity in the mosaic or melting pot of North American society, and especially by encouraging students not to link their own situation to those of such off-campus groups, a vision of overall institutional change and/or of social change will become vaguer. As a bonus, if this concept of "identity politics" can spread to the larger society, left-wing solidarity will be transformed from "how can your group and my group mutually aid each other to achieve a common beneficial change?" to "how can your group ensure that my group attains everything it wants?" Lack of solidarity also makes large national activist organizations (coalitions) impossible, whether of dissident students, faculty, or members of the public. Fracturing the opposition is always a good plan for maintaining the status quo. This aspect of the new mind-set can build on how Negro and women's liberation leaders often are quicker to denounce participants in movements for social change for perceived shortcomings than to protest effectively against the laws or customs that these leaders feel constrain the advancement of members of their groups.

- Alter students' sense of history as consisting of an agreed-upon progression of events to, as Matthew Arnold called it, a "huge Mississippi of falsehood" (Bartlett 622). Marxism, which has definitely influenced student protesters' view of past, present and future, claims that history demonstrates that revolution is inevitable: that "oppression" by capitalists will lead to their overthrow by employees. If students' belief in history as a series of events, each with a cause and a consequence, can be undermined, not only will the attraction of Marxism be lessened for them. Lack of a common historical sense also will aid in the fracturing of solidarity mentioned in the previous bulleted item:

each splinter of society will be free to construct its own version of the past, complete with its menu of grievances and demands. The resultant endless arguments between splinters that naturally will follow will help ensure that a common front to work toward fundamental social change is unlikely.

• Mock and/or denounce students' empathy for the downtrodden. The challenge here is to induce students to abandon any feeling of kinship with the less fortunate at home and abroad. Such fellow-feeling can lead to a desire to do something to change the unfortunates' situation and hence represents a first step toward activism. This stance can be attacked as slumming, or as imposing alien values on people who are probably perfectly happy in their poverty or in what can be misrepresented as misfortune. Students must be convinced that their attempt to understand others' social situation, and especially to communicate to the wider world something of another group's attitudes, beliefs, accomplishments, etc., is a form of theft—stealing the existential essence of such a group. Since young people can have an initial negative response to learning that others lack privileges they enjoy, such impulsive empathy can in the last resort be neutralized to irony. Irony is a stance young people find attractive—after all, it presupposes a sense of superiority toward what the ironist gazes upon (that which is gazed at does not realize its shortcomings the way the ironist does). Facilitating students' adoption of irony as an attitude toward the world encourages them to safely distance themselves from others' perceived predicaments. Likely students will feel equal distance from the established systems that at present structure society, but with such distance comes a declining inclination to try to alter those structures.

Besides the above parameters necessary for the success of the new on-campus mind-set, our professor realizes that for this cluster of concepts to be effective it must also include:

- Language taken from the vocabulary of left-wing opposition. Adherents of the new approach need to believe their scholarly, creative and pedagogical activities based on these ideas are revolutionary, in keeping with what they consider to be the spirit of the age and/or a moral imperative, even while the adoption of these concepts restores the campuses to their pacific, detached, time-honoured role. By transforming (reducing or eliminating the political content of) and adopting words such as "radical," "innovative," "subversive," "nontraditional," and "resistance," the new slate of attitudes can convince students they are still functioning in a "progressive" oppositional milieu.
- Language that sounds science-y, even while science is denounced. Marxists speak of "scientific socialism," and science is generally believed to be the fountainhead of truth. Hence science must be described in such a way that its claims to veracity are undermined. This is in accordance with the basic tenet of inducing students to believe that nothing is true. Science can be declared suspect as a source of knowledge because it is a product of human beings, who naturally have their biases, and some examples can always be evoked of silly or stupid or wrong-headed scientific claims from the past. Science students know that in fact scientific theories are based on the results of reproducible experiments—experiments that can be repeated with the same results by anybody with any sort of bias anywhere in the world. So this new mind-set is unlikely to gain much purchase among science students or professors. Such a shortcoming is not a serious flaw, however, since most campus protest originates with humanities and social sciences students (the latter field known as the "soft sciences," where the scientific method is not rigorously followed). Yet students' general belief in the efficacy of science is unlikely to vanish entirely. Thus some science vocabulary must be employed: a specific stance toward primary material in literary criticism or anthropology, say, can be designated a "theory," or a confusing compositional strategy in fiction or poetry can be called "experimental."

- Language that substitutes new words for concepts already described by familiar words. This facet of the new approach is in accordance with the goal of hampering communication between students and the wider public. For instance, "subaltern" can be substituted for "subordinate," or "interrogate" for "question." A discussion of how complex an idea is can be said to "complicate" that idea. If a sample of writing is incomprehensible, its goal can be described as "to disrupt" or "to trouble" or "to subvert" ordinary syntax or interpretation. Rather than stating an author or instructor "focuses" or "concentrates" on a subject or viewpoint, if the latter need to be disparaged the statement can be made that the author or teacher "privileges" that subject or point of view. The negative connotations around the word "privilege" is a bonus beyond mere jargonization—the linking of a negative aura to the situation being described is a psychological step toward inducing the reader or listener to regard an action, idea or person with reduced credence.
- A distrust of language itself. Since written or spoken language is the means of communicating ideas, activist students will be less eager to articulate their beliefs to peers or the wider population if they can be persuaded to mistrust or dislike language per se. To this end, latent antiauthoritarianism can be evoked by claiming that grammar—which it is possible to portray as an array of rules undemocratically imposed on people by their language—intrinsically is oppressive. Once history and science (in this case, philology, child development, cognition studies, neurobiology) are disparaged sufficiently in students' minds, language can be denounced as inherently hierarchical, and hence racist, sexist, etc.
- Appeals to authority under the guise of antiauthoritarianism. Activist students who proclaim themselves antiauthoritarian nevertheless frequently quote dicta of Mao or Che Guevara or other revolutionary leaders as authorization for a political position or action. Similarly, students can be induced to reflexively respect authority by insisting they justify their views, however

supposedly contrarian, by reference to or quotation from a pre-approved selection of notable contributors to the new slate of ideas. Encouraging this stricture not only channels a student's thinking into prescribed paths, it also blunts critical thinking that can lead to unsound conclusions by requiring reference to a precedent (proof that an idea is already sanctioned by an authority) for any opinion.

- A career path. Real revolution creates an uncertain future, even for revolutionaries. While young people love to regard themselves as adventurous, most attend college or university with the solid expectation of bettering their social and/or economic prospects in the long run. Ensuring that those students who adopt the new mind-set are rewarded with academic jobs—indeed, making proof of an applicant's familiarity and facility with this new collection of concepts a *requirement* for academic employment—will help ensure the widespread acceptance of these precepts.

The bulleted wish lists above will be instantly recognizable to anyone who has spent time in certain contemporary university departments as the essence of postmodernist thought. Of course, postmodernism was not adopted by postsecondary professors, programs, and departmental and course syllabi at the urging of one conservative professor, or even a cabal of the same. Yet campus unrest was at its height toward the end of the 1960s when North American academics in the humanities and social sciences began to absorb and promulgate the ideas of the linguists, philosophers, psychologists, cultural anthropologists and critics whose writings constitute postmodernist beliefs.

And as these ideas were embraced by many professors, and passed along to their students, campuses were indeed transformed. Postsecondary institutions changed from functioning as lively centres of unbridled inquiry and protest from which young people fanned out to build local and national anti-Vietnam War, anti-imperialist, anti-racist social movements, and to help raise and expand society's consciousness about feminism and ecology. Such student engagement with the larger society—whose taxes fund academic life—had been leading, as our professor noted, toward a realization by activist students that how employment is organized enables the daily reproduction of the systems of production and consumption that keep in power the hierarchies that benefit most from capitalism and its handmaidens, global commerce and war.

Today, with postmodernism a significant mode of thought in many humanities and social science disciplines, English-speaking universities and colleges have become placid degree mills where students meekly undergo training in accepting a lifetime of personal debt and in accepting the immutability of existing economic and social arrangements. As governments have dropped the goal of extending postsecondary education to an ever-larger percentage of the population, except with reference to "job skills training," universities have become increasingly corporatized in terms of funding, self-image, and structure. Despite the self-proclaimed "left-wing" content of postmodernist ideas, faculty have almost as meekly as students acceded to the extension of corporate influence over the priorities and conduct of postsecondary institutions. For all the tens of thousands of classroom lectures, assigned textbooks, academic articles, and student papers filled with anti-capitalist rhetoric, no effective national organization exists in North America of professors or students actively confronting corporate influence on- or off-campus.

All is calm on the campuses, except for flare-ups of the office politics that affect every large hierarchical enterprise. Where faculty unions exist, they do blunt the worst excesses of management. But in the absence of social-change unionism, faculty unions, like the rest of the current trade union movement, are essentially labour brokers and enforcers of the labour truce represented by collective agreements.

II

That postmodernist beliefs constitute a conservative initiative, aimed at pacifying campus and community alike, is no secret (except perhaps to some of its adherents), as a few examples below will illustrate.

And postmodernism at its core exhibits enough contradictions, inconsistencies, absurdities and outright falsehoods (despite its protective insistence that nothing is true) to ensure that its impact on academia and literature will not ultimately endure. An exploration of three significant examples of these flaws as they relate to the study and creation of literature—the main focus of the present paper—follows the evidence below of a wide awareness of the reactionary nature of this slate of beliefs. But first, for any reader unfamiliar with the mind-set, a definition and examples will briefly be offered.

The magisterial dean of literary definition, M.H. Abrams, states that postmodernism is a term frequently applied to post-World War II literature and art. "Postmodernism," he specifies, "involves not only a continuation, sometimes carried to an extreme, of the countertraditional experiments of modernism, but also diverse attempts to break away from modernist forms which had, inevitably, become in their turn conventional" (176). Abrams adds that an intent of postmodernist authors is also "to overthrow the elitism of modernist 'high art' by recourse for models to the 'mass culture' in film, television, newspaper cartoons, and popular music." He says postmodern literature often "blend[s] literary genres, cultural and stylistic levels, the serious and the playful" and therefore such writing does not easily fit into traditional literary classification. Abrams includes literature of the absurd in his description of the aim of some postmodernist authors "to subvert the foundations of our accepted modes of thought and experience so as to reveal the meaninglessness of existence." He thus links literary postmodernism to the poststructuralist approach in linguistic and literary theory, observing that poststructuralists

> undertake to subvert the foundations of language in order to demonstrate that its seeming meaningfulness dissipates, for a rigorous inquirer, into a play of conflicting indeterminacies, or else undertake to show that all forms of cultural discourse are manifestations of the reigning ideology, or of the relations and constructions of power, in contemporary society. (177)

Student or faculty postmodernist literary criticism in practice involves obligatory reference to a narrow band of critics and philosophers. In a characterization that applies to many of these thinkers' works, Stuart Sim describes the efforts of one of the presiding figures of postmodernist criticism, Jacques Lacan (1901-1981), as "notoriously difficult to interpret" (68). No essay, thesis or journal article would be regarded as complete (or whose arguments would be considered as sound) without at least a nod to French philosopher Jacques Derrida (1930-2004). Citation of at least one pensée of Derrida's replaces the absolutely required reference in literary essays, theses and articles during the 1940s through 1970s to at least one critical precept of Anglo-American poet *and* critic T.S. Eliot (1888-1965).

Besides Lacan and Derrida, other critics who can be invoked include Viktor Shklovsky (1893-1984), Mikhail Bakhtin (1895-1975), Roland Barthes (1915-1980), Jean-François Lyotard (1924-1998), Michel Foucault (1926-1984), Luce Irigaray (b. 1932), Hélène Cixious (b. 1937), Julia Kristeva (b. 1941), and Gayatri Chakravorty Spivak (b. 1942).

In courses, programs and departments where the postmodernist approach to literature is the dominant operational guide, the ideas of these approved authorities are called "theories." As our professor yearned for in 1970, this science-y term is applied to the notions of the critics and philosophers without being accompanied by any of the rest of the accoutrements of actual science: the articulation of a clear hypothesis, the development of experiments capable of testing the theory, reproducible results, control groups, and so on. But for students in such courses and programs, the ability to adroitly reference these "theories" is vital for academic success. "The final mark for one's work," Sim observes, "will reflect the degree of success in articulating, and then applying, the theoretical 'line' as much as anything else. The last thing one wants is to be accused of in such situations is being 'undertheorized'—that way, low marks lie" (10).

Contemporary poetry regarded as postmodern consists of writing that is paratactic—that is, the grammatical and logical connections between words, phrases and concepts are frequently missing. The writing is determinedly nonnarrative, nonrepresentational and nonlinear, and is essentially conceptual art: the ideas or feelings that the piece is meant to convey are of negligible value compared to the cleverness/obliqueness of the artist's chosen method to present her or his subject matter. Often a compositional strategy of accretion or collage is employed.

For example, here are the first four stanzas of "Any Publicity Is Good Publicity" by Mark Wallace, co-editor of *Telling It Slant: Avant-Garde Poetics of the 1990s* (University of Alabama Press, 2001):

> Won't have to testify about
> pigs guilty on the rotunda. Get packing
> nomad street misunderstanding
>
> in second gear. Catch today
> impersonating tomorrow. Down under
> phone static, what's worth
>
> being a cleaner health inspector
> not wearing a hat? Screwed
> on the cola marriage circuit
>
> and the power's up for gripes
> about who calls who.
> Show me your badge again. (82)

Or here are the first three stanzas from "Summer Triangle" by derek beaulieu, poet laureate of Calgary 2014-16:

> four southern regions
>
> rocks leave their own images levels allow left
> & left & the & the mad dash *em* or a single
> feather
>
> birdman points to one grotto (15)

In its entirety, here is "Banish" by Margaret Christakos, University of Windsor's writer-in-residence 2004-2005:

> Banished. Abdehins. Ba ni sh ed. De. Hs. In. Ab.
> B_____d.
> _anishe_.
> __nish__.
> __is___.
> Ban_hed.
> _an_he_.
> _a__hed.
> _a_sh_d.
> ____sh__.
> Ba_____d.
> ____she_.
> _____he_.
> B_____e_. (49)

Billy Collins, U.S. poet laureate 2001-2003, characterizes such poems in the Introduction to his poetry anthology *180 More* (Random House, 2005) as fundamentally unwelcoming to readers. A clearly written poem can be difficult to interpret, Collins argues, but that is not the same as a poem that immediately blocks its readers' access. "If you need to cut an entrance into a poem, who is going to bother?" he asks (xvi). "If a poem has no clear starting place," he continues, "how can it go anywhere? If a poem does not begin in lucidity, how can it advance into the mysterious" (xvi)? As an example of an unwelcoming start to a poem, he picks the opening lines of a poem, "Up to Speed," by postmodernist Rae Armantrout, whose collection *Versed* won the 2010 Pulitzer Prize:

> Streamline to instantaneous
> voucher in / voucher out
> system. (xv)

Armantrout is associated with the postmodernist literary faction known as the "Language" poets, after one of their publishing venues in the 1970s, a magazine entitled *L=A=N=G=U=A=G=E*. Language poetry operates from the premise, according to the Academy of American Poets, "that language dictates meaning rather than the other way around" (Academy). Language poetry also requires "reader participation in the construction of meaning" (Academy). Critic Robert von Hallberg, in an essay more sympathetic to this kind of writing than Collins, tackles a poem by Language poet Michael Palmer. Palmer served as a chancellor of the Academy of American Poets 1999-2004, and in 2006 was awarded the Academy's $100,000 Wallace Stevens Award. The first six lines of his "Construction of the Museum" are:

In the hole we found beside the road
something would eventually go

Names we saw spelled backward there

In the sand we found a tablet

In the hole caused by bombs
which are smart we might find a hand (von Hallberg 187)

The concept that the reader must construct meaning from such an apparently-baffling collection of clauses and phrases does not allow, von Hallberg argues, the poem to mean anything any reader unilaterally decides it does, "though this naïve sort of populism is often adduced to support the poetic policies of Language writing" (187). For von Hallberg, the compositional strategy of a poem such as Palmer's points to "a structure, or poem, behind the poem; the words on the page evoke a poem beyond the page, one that isn't there, strictly speaking" (186). Poems like Palmer's "imply that there is a structure behind the text …, a coherence beyond the surface incoherence or disjunctiveness of the words, lines, or stanzas on the page" (187). Von

Hallberg traces this approach to poetry back to the U.S. poet Ezra Pound (1885-1972; see below for more on postmodernists' continual evocation of Pound): "Pound's enormous idealism rested on a faith that the structuring powers of the mind are universal, natural, and effective at identifying orders not marked by the conjunctions that conventionally indicate intellectual relations: if, then, but, because, for, although, however, and so on" (187). Palmer's parataxis, von Hallberg insists, works because of the coherent poem behind the poet's apparently incoherent one: "The gap between normative English syntax and Palmer's syntax itself identifies a utopian conceptual space for the poem: there is an order elsewhere, beyond the page" (188). The critic claims the "elsewhere" he identifies, wherein the "hypothetical coherence" (190) of Palmer's poem may be found, "resides in conventions established historically in an interpretive community" (188), that is, the conventions employed by ordinary readers of English.

This torturous extraction of coherence from apparent incoherence is necessary, or even to be desired, according to von Hallberg, because "I look to poetry for an extension of conventional patterns of thinking" (190). Yet "patterns of thinking" surely have a cultural and/or neurobiological—hardly a poetic—origin. Moreover, why such an "extension" is necessary or desirable is not discussed by the critic. Nor why poetry, of all human endeavours, should be singled out to bear the burden of this enormous task of mental realignment. Even if poetry were the best route to this goal, von Hallberg does not explain why a particular *form*—specifically, writing that is unintelligible to an average reader—is the preferred route to extend patterns of thought, as opposed to, for instance, bringing to literature new *content*. One thinks of how feminist poetry with a clearly accessible message—witty, poignant, biting, denunciatory—as part of a burgeoning social movement helped change people's once-conventional thinking about the roles and status of women. And many scholars such as Marshall McLuhan (cf. *The Gutenberg Galaxy*) have made the case that changes in technology—the invention and adoption of certain tools or machines and the resultant economic and social changes that accompany the integration of such tools or machines into society—is actually how von Hallberg's "conventional patterns of thinking" are altered (Grady 14, 24-25), rather than via poetry.

Although for postmodernists poetry is expected to be unwelcoming to a reader—to depart from "normative English syntax" in von Hallberg's words—the same is not usually expected of prose, however. One hears from postmodernist practitioners and advocates several reasons for employing parataxis (reasons included in our professor's 1970 wish list).

Especially invoked is the assertion that conventional language use, involving rules of grammar and logical construction of thought, is bad (authoritarian, racist, sexist, patriarchal, imperialist, homophobic, etc.). But the defense of parataxis, and the denunciation of conventional English usage is presented using, er, conventional English usage. With prose, the only nod to the supposed crimes and shortcomings of language is found in the frequent turbidity of postmodernist critical essays, with heavy use of jargon substituting for clarity of idea.

In an era when cosmologist-authors such as Brian Greene, Stephen Hawking and Steven Weinberg can offer lucid discussions of such complex esoterica as post-Big-Bang inflation, string theory, and dark matter, the murkiness of much critical writing about postmodern literature is startling. Here is Jon Paul Fiorentino, editor-in-chief of Concordia University's *Matrix* literary magazine, introducing his collection of postmodern prairie poetry: "These are poets who unwrite the prairie. I suppose it is not enough to say they are immersed in immersion. The idea of descriptive poetics (as opposed to prescriptive) is key. ... The anxiety of geography is reshaping the context" (9). What the anthologist means by "unwriting" a geography, or what an author being "immersed in immersion" means, or the difference between "descriptive" and "prescriptive" poetics, or what the "anxiety of geography" refers to is nowhere discussed. Apparently a mere mention of these concepts, which evidently the reader is meant to be appreciative of or to be awed by rather than to understand, is sufficient. This approach pervades Fiorentino's explanation of his book, for example: "If the previous prairie ethic/aesthetic relied on notions of found linguistic material (as opposed to received linguistic material), of an extrapolation of vernacular (as opposed to idiom), of reproaching universality (as opposed to approaching universality), then this project [the anthology] necessarily becomes an extension of that ethic as well as a response" (10).

Missing from any defense of postmodernist approaches to literature is a consideration of the *politics* of obfuscation in literary creation and criticism: who benefits when comprehension of an art form, or of a critical discussion of that art form, is narrowed to an academically trained cohort assigned to, or willing to, attempt the interpretation of deliberately obscure writing? Postmodernists' intentional creation of obstacles to understanding by the larger public or audience for such writing indicates a tendency for postmodernism's practitioners to regard themselves as an elite—whether these obstacles consist of compositional strategies utilized in artistic endeavours, or of heavy employment of jargon and idiosyncratic redefinition of common words in gestures to explain the merits of such art. Restriction of cultural knowledge to a(n) (elite) few is a conservative agenda, essentially reactionary in that it harkens back to a time before an educated, involved populace was a proclaimed goal of democratically governed communities.

As mentioned above, awareness that these postmodern beliefs and practice are a tool for conservative social control is no secret, and not just among students, scholars and practitioners of the literary arts. Writing in the *Globe and Mail*, cultural critic Ian Buruma describes the wholehearted adoption by U.S. Tea Party Republicans of the first item on our professor's 1970 wish list: to instil a belief that nothing is true. Demonstration by experts of the falsehood of statements by former Republican senator Rick Santorum[1] had no impact on his followers, Buruma notes, because like postmodernists, Santorum's constituency insists that objective truth does not exist.

---

1 Santorum, who was seeking to become the Republicans' presidential nominee, had said that ten per cent of all deaths in the Netherlands are caused by euthanasia, with half of these killings imposed on patients against their will. He further claimed that the elderly in Holland are so frightened by the situation that they now wear bracelets asking not to be euthanized.

> The first people to argue that all truth is relative, and that all information is a form of propaganda that reflects society's power relations, were far removed from the world inhabited by Mr. Santorum and his supporters. Several decades ago, a number of European and U.S. intellectuals, often with a background in Marxism, developed a 'postmodern' critique of the written word. We might think, they argued, that what we read in *The New York Times* or *Le Monde* is objectively true, but everything that appears there is, in fact, a disguised form of propaganda for bourgeois class interests. There's no such thing, the postmodern critic believes, as independence of thought. Objective truth is an illusion. … The real lie, in this view, is the claim of objectivity.

Buruma notes that followers of Santorum who dismiss, for example, the *Washington Post*'s conclusion that "there was 'not a shred of evidence' to back up Mr. Santorum's claims" are perfect postmodernists. "The most faithful followers of obscure leftist thinkers in Paris, New York or Berkeley," Buruma concludes, "are the most reactionary elements in the American heartland."

Postmodernism's "nothing is true" is used as well by employers and real estate speculators to try to neutralize employee or community resistance via a process called "narrative capture." Where employees of an enterprise are proving troublesome—seeking better wages or conditions, or upset by some new management scheme—narrative capture experts are employed to conduct interviews with employees concerning the issue or issues being contested. The resulting study may be presented as an attempt to document the "work culture" of the enterprise. Subsequently, at a meeting of employees the various responses to these interviews are offered, along with management's position. Employees are assured that, via narrative capture, management has listened to their perspective. But since there is no truth, only "competing narratives," employees are informed that their individual view of the flashpoint issue is only one possible way of seeing the situation, of no more or less value than any other. Employees are urged to see management's viewpoint as equally valid as their own expression of a sense of injustice. The hope is that employees will agree that since, after all, management is charged with controlling the enterprise, management's narrative concerning the situation should prevail, and employees should abandon their struggle to improve their working lives. Alternatively, management learns to "spin" their take on a situation in order to refute or defuse the dissatisfactions that inform their employees' narratives (TMiller).

Similarly, a real estate speculator meeting resistance from the community will hire a narrative capture expert, who interviews community members regarding their opposition to some proposed real estate initiative. At a community meeting, the various "competing narratives" are presented. Community members are urged to see that their vision of how their community might develop is only one possible scenario. Since the speculator's view of the situation is held to be equally valid with the perspective of community members opposed to the speculator's plans, and since the speculator is going to "invest" in the community, the hope of the speculator is to thereby undermine community resistance, community solidarity.

Adherence to other postmodernist precepts also results in the mindset's followers reinforcing right-wing values. Reviewing Bruce Robbins' *Upward Mobility and the Common Good* (Princeton University Press, 2007), Portland State University's Jennifer Ruth notes Robbins' claim that Foucault's opposition to the state leads to a misunderstanding of contemporary power relations. Ruth continues:

> Appalled by neoliberal cutting-and-slashing, many leftist critics nonetheless continue to churn out Foucaultian monographs, as if there were no possible relationship between a discourse suspicious of state services and one dismantling such services. In a startling but effective move, Robbins places Foucault not in his usual company of Derrida and Lacan ... but of social conservatives like Christopher Lasch who see the rise of a professionally-administered state as an assault on individual accountability and self-reliance. Robbins writes, "The complicity of

Foucaultian antistatism with Republican free-market enthusiasm for privatization should give pause even to those who are most likely to be skeptical of expanding state surveillance and intervention." (168)

The equivalence of the postmodernist ethos and the beliefs of religious conservatives is explored by bioarchaeologist Gordon Rakita, writing in the Society for Archaeological Science's *SAS Bulletin*. He decries the "postmodern philosophical underpinnings of the intelligent design movement ... [and] the commonalities between the critiques of evolutionary theory offered by creationists and many radical postmodernist scholars" (25). The creationist and postmodernist movements both "make the rejection of scientific claims and evolutionary science itself a part of their primary goals," Rakita says. "For those of us who take part in the scientific enterprise or who teach science, such attacks offer constant distractions and distortions."

Raikita then introduces and disproves six "common arguments posed by radical postmodernists and creationists," including: that evolution and Social Darwinism are equivalent, that evolution leads to immorality and denies spirituality and human agency, that evolution asserts all change is random, and that evolution does not explain everything. He states that these arguments surface regularly in academia, and that science professors "often confront one version (the creationist) in our classrooms, only to have to face the other (the post-modern) in our faculty meetings. The consistency and consonance of their criticisms is ironic" (26).

The absurdity of postmodernism's warped depictions of the scientific process was most famously underlined by a hoax perpetrated by New York University's Alan Sokol in 1996. Ecocritic Harold Fromm, writing in *The Hudson Review*, quotes Sokol as saying that in the 1990s he became aware of "the phenomenon of postmodernist literary intellectuals pontificating on science and its philosophy and making a complete bungle of both. I decided to write a parody of postmodern science criticism, to see whether it could get accepted as a serious scholarly article in a trendy academic journal" (Fromm 574).

The eventual article "Transgressing the Boundaries: Towards a Transformative Hermeneutics of Quantum Gravity" (Sim 13) was accepted by *Social Text*, "a politically correct cultural studies journal of the left," in Fromm's designation (574), and published in their Spring/ Summer 1996 issue. Among other "lunatic" (Sim 13) assertions, Sokol's article proclaims that the value of pi (π) is not constant but relative to an observer's position. Such extreme relativism has been, as Fromm observes, "increasingly adopted by the conservative anti-Darwinian, Intelligent Design right" (574). He details a New York University philosopher's account of a postmodernist archaeologist who declares, "Science is just one of many ways of knowing the world. [The cosmological myth of an American aboriginal tribe] is just as valid as the archaeological viewpoint of what prehistory is about" (575). Fromm observes that "the connections of this [claim] to the Intelligent Design movement need hardly be pressed" (575).

Fromm, always conscious of the ecological crisis that is occurring concurrently with postmodernism's attacks on science, reports that one former postmodernist anti-science crusader, Bruno Latour, about 2004 had a change of heart.

> Powerfully cognizant of the way in which right-wing fundamentalism and politics have mastered only too well the debunking *mentalité* of "*critique*"—denial of global warming, endorsement of Intelligent Design, anti-science evasions of law and sideswipings of constitutionality to promulgate a war and reward the super-rich—Latour reversed gears (with a vengeance). (578)

Fromm quotes Latour:

> While we spent years trying to detect the real prejudices hidden behind the appearance of objective statements, do we now have to reveal the real objective and incontrovertible facts hidden behind the *illusion* of prejudices? And yet entire Ph.D. programs are still running to make sure that

> good American kids are learning the hard way that facts
> are made up, that there is no such thing as natural, unme-
> diated, unbiased access to truth, that we are always pris-
> oners of language, that we always speak from a particular
> standpoint, and so on, while dangerous extremists are using
> the very same argument of social construction to destroy
> hard-won evidence that could save our lives. (Fromm 578)

The reactionary implications of other postmodernist tenets, beyond denial of objective truth and hence the truths of science, have been identified, for example in an appraisal of identity politics. Reviewing the course of contemporary feminism, *The New Yorker*'s Ariel Levy says that "[a] politics of liberation was largely supplanted by a politics of identity" (80). Levy argues that:

> if feminism becomes a politics of identity, it can safely be
> drained of ideology. Identity politics isn't much concerned
> with abstract ideals, like justice. It's a version of the old spoils
> system: align yourself with other members of a group—
> Irish, Italian, women, or whatever—and try to get a bigger
> slice of the resources that are being allocated. If a demand for
> revolution is tamed into a simple insistence on representa-
> tion, then one woman is as good as another. You could have,
> in a sense, feminism without feminists. You could have, for
> example, … [former Alaska governor and U.S. Tea Party
> Republican vice-presidential candidate] Sarah Palin." (80)

Responding to an overview of Canadian postmodern poetry by Pauline Butling and Susan Rudy, *Writing in Our Time: Canada's Radical Poetries in English (1957-2003)*, Brock University's Gregory Betts takes issue with the authors' postmodernist appropriation of the term "radical" to define the writing of the authors the book focuses on:

> [T]he idea of a "radical" author as presented in this study
> bears little outward resemblance to the political tradition

of radicalism. For instance, the enshrinement of the TISH
writers [a group of young poets studying at the University
of B.C. in the mid-1960s, loosely grouped around the journal *Tish*] into the mainstream body of Canadian literature
presents more of a contradiction to the book's rhetoric of
antagonistic marginality than either Butling or Rudy admit
in any of their essays: a contradiction that continues in
their extensive list of other radical poets—including such
"marginal" writers (144) as Robert Kroetsch (10), George
Bowering, Margaret Atwood, Michael Ondaatje, Daphne
Marlatt (23), bpNichol (24), Roy Miki (26), and Christian
Bök (73). What brings these writers together is not cultural
marginality, or even radical activity (in the conventional
use of the term to refer to far leftist political agitation). ...
[T]he radical writers mapped out in this book participate in
the contemporary Canadian literary mainstream; they are
all amongst the most taught, hired, awarded and celebrated
of contemporary Canadian authors, and have all consis-
tently been beneficiaries of governmental subsidies. (24-25)

Obviously, calling the mainstream "radical" drains the meaning
from both terms, and aids the conservative project of confusing students and others regarding the politically oppositional nature of a
radical stance, activity, or organization.

Specialized (including debased, as in the deployment of "radical")
use of ordinary words, along with jargon (such as "implicated" in the
following quotation), are partly why some academics question the
project of much contemporary literary criticism. Markus Poetzsch of
Wilfrid Laurier University muses that a polished critical article can
hide a contemporary scholar's doubts and worries,

worries that what we labour to produce after countless hours
of research, grant applications and social isolation will only
ever be read by a handful of specialists and the occasional
harassed student, worries that the non-academic public is

really not interested (or shall we say *implicated*) in these texts, does not seek them out, and would in all likelihood be confused, bored or irritated if invited to read them. Still more troubling is the thought that even academics do not invariably enjoy reading the texts produced by other specialists, colleagues or students; we are not, or at least not often enough, moved by them or bettered in any appreciable way. (128)

Poetzsch quotes the University of London scholar Chris Baldick as stating that contemporary literary studies may at their worst "proliferate impenetrable jargon, produce gluts of unwanted articles, jump aboard theoretical bandwagons, or disappear into arcane specialization" (128). The rewards for this behaviour, Poetzsch notes, "are by no means paltry": tenure and promotion. But the academy's present overwhelming emphasis on "interpretive innovation or distinctiveness" (129) is market-driven, he says, a manoeuvre necessary for increased academic status rather than an activity intended to produce insights that might benefit readers. A critical endeavour required by the current academic marketplace frequently is "not interested in notions of 'truth' or 'validity' (however complexly these may be framed, articulated or positioned for debate) and in fact makes its object the perpetual deferment of these more traditional goals in order to ensure untrammelled interpretive freedom" (129).

Such desperately unique responses to literature "[begin] to take on the … 'fabricated' nature of literature itself" (129). Poetzsch refers to philosopher Emmanuel Levinas' characterization of "'the vanity of fabricating books'" (128), and adds:

Not only do [critics] write (at the best of times) for a numerically limited readership and one, moreover, that is in some sense complicit in the economy of vanity and fabrication, but we do so without a clear sense of, or appreciable regard for, that audience's needs and interests. Literary criticism is, after all, driven primarily by authorial and institutional needs, not by the needs of its anticipated (and unanticipated) readership. (130)

III

Far from meeting reader's needs, postmodernist ideas, like the creative works they extoll, function instead as agents of social repression, furthering a reactionary agenda as the above examples of this mind-set in practice demonstrate. But even if literary postmodernism were a neutral or even progressive influence on the academy and society, the mind-set embraces a number of claims and concepts that do not withstand scrutiny (in addition to the idea that there is no truth, and that therefore science perpetuates falsehoods). Three central literary postmodern assertions are:

- **Postmodern poetry is avant-garde, innovative, and experimental, and forces its readers to think in new ways.**

"Avant-garde" delineates the forefront of a military advance, behind which the massed forces of an army must follow. But the writing called (often self-designatedly) "avant-garde" has so far in literary history been a tangential approach to literary practice, rather than a forerunner or harbinger of the direction literature will take. After four decades of postmodern "theory" and practice of poetry, for example, a glance at the majority of North American literary journals and published collections of poems is ample evidence of postmodernism's minor influence in the creative realm. Postmodernism is, then, whatever its influence on literary criticism or the social sciences, incidental to the main developments in poetry over the past forty years. An article in the *Literary History of Saskatchewan* by the author of this essay notes:

> Non-referential, non-linear writing began in 1915 with the rise of the Dada and then surrealist art movements. Around this time, free verse began to challenge as the defining characteristic of poetry the use of regular patterns of sound (rhyme), rhythm (metre), and stanza. However, whereas free verse blazed the trail most poets since have followed, non-referential, non-linear writing has never been the vanguard of poetic expression, but remains a minority offshoot. (115)

The so-called "avant-garde" is more like a detachment or squad that has wandered away from the main body of the army until out of communication range of the rest of the troops, albeit singing martial songs and shouting fierce slogans by way of keeping up its courage. The lost platoon's self-bestowed title is a masterwork of spin, like that of real estate speculators who trash natural environments or existing neighbourhoods for profit but call themselves "developers." As Columbia University's Edward Mendelson points out in an article on New York School poet Frank O'Hara (1926-1966):

> Avant-gardes claim to create the art of the future. But the "art of the future" generally proves wrong about the real future of art in the same way that the "city of the future" on display at a world's fair proves wrong about the future of cities. ... [Nineteenth-century French poet Charles] Baudelaire dismissed the avant-garde as a "military metaphor": until the mid-nineteenth century the word meant only the front ranks of an army. The avant-garde idea was suitable only to "those who can only think collectively" ("que ne peuvent penser qu'en société"), not to those for whom ... the only truth is face to face. An avant-garde coterie always prefers a revolution in language and technique to a revelation of thought and feeling. O'Hara recognized this preference as a sign of insecurity, a failure of nerve. (34)

Mendelson quotes O'Hara as mocking the belief in the artistic and literary circles in which he ran that anything excellent "must surely be avant-garde because whatever is avant-garde is also excellent," stating in a humorous poem: "[I]t's new, it must be vanguard!"

Curiously, the insistence among postmodernism's advocates that writers who believe in the cause must be "avant-garde" or "cutting-edge" means these critics have adopted a linear terminology, a linear metaphor. Linear thinking is ordinarily a negative among postmodernists. This apparently is due to believers expanding the opposition of philosopher Jean-François Lyotard to "metanarratives"—sweeping overviews of history that, for instance, describe the rise of political democracy or the colonization of North America as inevitable, a series of steps considered progress toward a goal (Sim 97-98). From regarding all grand narratives with suspicion, the next step was to question and reject any articulation of a sequenced development: linear thinking. Except, obviously, when perception of such a sequence bolsters postmodern claims, such as that paratactic writers are out in front of a mass of all other dutiful follower-writers, or that paratactic writing is the sharp edge of a blade—the rest of the blade consisting of the literature that trails behind the writing that constitutes the working forefront of the art. (Another authorized departure from nonlinear thinking is that postmodernism is not a singular cultural event but is rather a direct successor of/improvement upon modernism.)

The term "innovative" as applied to contemporary paratactic art is as dubious a designation as "avant-garde." After a century of parataxis, there is nothing novel or groundbreaking about yet another work that fractures grammar or a logical sequence of thought. The only way in which parataxis is innovative is identical to how, for example, every poet not utilizing traditional regular patterns of sound, rhythm and stanza is innovative in what he or she creates: with the advent of free verse, the poet invents the art form each time he or she writes a poem. Decisions regarding lineation, indents, margins, white space, punctuation and more must be settled by the free verse poet each time a new work is crafted. And free-verse poets drawing on image banks new to the art form, bringing new content (subject matter) into poetry, or incorporating a vocabulary not previously found in poetry are also innovators. What good poem of whatever critical school is not innovative in some way? In reality, "innovative" is a synonym for "well-crafted" when it comes to contemporary poetry: every good poem engages us with a surprising aspect to diction, form and/or content (although surprise alone does not guarantee literary accomplishment). The only non-innovative poems are those employing clichés of diction, form or content, and such poems can equally be postmodern or free verse.

"Experimental" is as misleading an adjective for postmodern poetry as "innovative," except for a similar acknowledgement that *all* effective authors of every literary tradition continually experiment—rethink, recast, revise a piece of writing—in order to shape the best possible vehicle to convey their artistic intent. Limiting the descriptor of "experimental" to paratactic poetry raises the implied question: what is the hypothesis the experiment is intending to test? Also: what is the result? As U.S. poet William Stafford (1914-1993), who in 1970 served as the Consultant in Poetry to the Library of Congress (the appointment now known as the U.S. Poet Laureate), says in an interview:

> I feel a lot of disquiet about the purposefully experimental. I mean purposeful anything. Purposefully patriotic, purposefully revolutionary, purposefully experimental, they're all leaving the center. They're all forsaking that inner compass that art comes from. The rest is artificial, drawing by the numbers. It disquiets me to see these blurbs on books. "This extends further." You know, the current trend of the experimental. I don't care where you're experimenting: what are you finding? What's there? (51)

Parataxis' original experiment was to test the conviction by adherents of Dada and surrealism that an encounter with examples of these artistic approaches would alter readers' and viewers' overall perception of the world, resulting in beneficial social change (specifically, the overthrow of the capitalist social order). The hypothesis was that exposure to literary and artistic nonreferentiality and nonlinearity would induce citizens to comprehend their society's fundamental flaws and the preferable alternative represented by socialism. "Surrealism: the communism of genius?" read one slogan issued by the Bureau of Surrealist Research on Paris' Rue de Grenelle in the 1920s (Hunt 86). In 1962, André Breton (1896-1966), a founder of surrealism, said of the movement's revolutionary beginnings:

> We felt that a run-down society, rushing towards its doom could only succeed in prolonging its existence by reinforcing its taboos and multiplying its constraints and we were

determined to defy them. But so far that determination had only been passive: now we were possessed by a desire to subvert everything. … During this period we were determined to reply in kind to a society which shocked and disgusted us. (Hunt 84)

But the political nature of surrealist art was central. A "Manifesto for Independent Revolutionary Art," supposedly written by Breton and Leon Trotsky in 1938 and signed by Breton and Mexican muralist Diego Rivera, states:

It should be clear by now that in defending freedom of thought we have no intention of justifying political indifference, and that it is far from our wish to revive a so-called pure art which generally serves the extremely impure ends of reaction. No, our conception of the role of art is too high to refuse it an influence on the fate of society. We believe that the supreme task of art in our epoch is to take part actively and consciously in the preparation of the revolution. (Breton)

Although similar claims are made by postmodernist literary practitioners—that paratactic writing will lead to a transformation in people's political thinking—in nearly a century there is absolutely no evidence that such writing has the desired effect. The experiment may be safely judged a complete failure. As I have observed in another essay, rather than surrealism and its artistic descendants leading to a better world,

surrealism of late has become the favoured mode of television advertising. The corporations endorse a non-linear, collagist approach—wrenching items out of their expected context, "defamiliarizing" them, as it were—in the hope of impressing on the viewer's imagination some new or improved product intended to be inflicted upon consumers.

> By way of contrast, mainstream lyric and anecdotal poetry has made a demonstrably useful contribution to social activism, providing inspiration and constituting a kind of documentary creative non-fiction. The river of mainstream poetry, rather than the self-lauded rivulet of the non-referential that accompanies it, has also borne into the art form's purview important new content not previously found there: aspects of women's lives, minority experiences, conditions and effects of how daily work is organized, and articulation of community life. (116)

One might expect that "experimental" postmodern writing would be enlisted to prove the validity of postmodernist literary "theories." But M.H. Abrams contrasts the concept of literary theory as ordinarily used and as postmodernism has appropriated the term, and shows why, despite the science-y language of postmodernism, no need is felt by its adherents to convincingly demonstrate the validity of a theory. "Since Plato and Aristotle," Abrams states, literary theory has been regarded as "a conceptual scheme, or set of principles, distinctions and categories—sometimes explicit, but often only implied in critical practice—for identifying, classifying, analyzing, and evaluating works of literature" (247). Postmodernist theory, however,

> often designates an account of the general conditions of signification that determine meaning and interpretation in all domains of human action, production and intellection. … As a consequence, the pursuit of literary criticism is conceived to be integral with all the other pursuits traditionally classified as the "human sciences," and to be inseparable from consideration of the general nature of human "subjectivity," and also from reference to all forms of social and cultural phenomena. Often the theory of signification is granted primacy in the additional sense that, when common experience in the use or interpretation of language does not accord with what the theory entails, such

experience is rejected as unjustified and illusory, or else is accounted an ideologically imposed concealment of the actual operation of the signifying system. (248)

Abrams does not mention that this practice of denouncing evidence that does not reinforce one's belief system—as he, in the preceding quote, observes postmodernists "often" do—is one of the main responses of people experiencing the mental affliction known as cognitive dissonance (McLeod). The critic *does* remark on the adversarial stance he calls a "prominent aspect" (Abrams 248) of postmodernist theories. Like surrealism's posture, the theories "are posed in opposition to inherited ways of thinking in all provinces of knowledge[:] … what they identify as the foundational assumptions, concepts, procedures, and findings in traditional modes of discourse in Western civilization (including literary criticism)" (248).

In an interview, Abrams refers to how this suspiciousness towards the wisdom of everything before postmodernism allows one to "look at old poems and come out with new readings" (Williams 78)—that academic-market-driven obsession with generating new interpretations of literature that Poetzsch refers to above. "I'm always suspicious of a theoretical construct that undertakes to persuade you that what people have always taken a poem to be about is not only wrong but the opposite of the truth," Abrams says. "That tends to be the paradigm for all sorts of recent theories of literature. … I've been skeptical from the beginning of all attempts to show that for hundreds of years people have been reading wrong, or have missed the real point" (Williams 78).

Meanwhile, one hears repeatedly from adherents that contemporary paratactic writing, composed like postmodernist literary theory in opposition to received concepts of written communication, effects a transformation in its readers' thought processes or political ideas by means of *force*. The recurrent claim is that parataxis "forces the reader" to think or undertake some other act. Oppressive political systems are to be denounced because they force an ideology and certain behaviours on the members of a society. But postmodern writing is good because it supposedly, er, forces readers to change their minds, to think henceforth in a better way. Yet, except in classrooms, and especially in graduate seminars, can anyone really be *forced* to think? Don't civilians, when faced with impenetrable texts, simply stop reading? And even in classrooms, do the afflicted really *think* about the material they face, or do they simply construct a response they hope will be acceptable to the authority figure who assigns their grade?

An example of how, against all common sense, we are informed repeatedly that postmodern writing *forces* readers to respond in a predetermined way to the incomprehensible text in front of them occurs in an interview in the literary journal *Contemporary Verse 2* with the Canadian postmodernist poet Rachel Zolf. The poet says:

> As Shoshana Felman writes, "The more a text is 'mad'—the more in other words it resists interpretation—the more its specific modes of resistance to reading become its 'subject' and its literarity." In other words, in all my books I try to enact situations where the reader feels uncomfortable, dislocated in their own skin, and is forced to think about why they feel that way. (Foster 10)

Answering the next question from the interviewer, Zolf speaks of a book by another author entirely "made from the words in a two-page legal document." When the book is read, Zolf says, "you are there with her ..., encaged in history, forced to think through what responsibility means" (Foster 11). Changing the verb slightly, Zolf speaks later of "the effects you can create by using beauty to draw and jar the reader into consciousness."

As ever with postmodernist assertions, no evidence is provided that, after reading a sample of paratactic writing, any reader engages in self-questioning, or adopts a changed value structure or political stance. Indeed, the contemporary postmodernist poet Jeff Derksen observes in a note on his poem "Forced Thoughts" that his title is "a term for a symptom of migraines in which the migraine sufferer is unable to shake a particular thought or progression of thoughts" (127). Derksen states that his poem is intended to echo a poem by a U.S.

poet that to Derksen manages "to uncannily capture and comment on [a] capitalist tension and its contradictions" (126); Derksen aims to, he says, "approach the contradictions of a particular social moment" (127). The poem begins:

> perceived accepted suffered
> merely naturally unites
> veils cultures call
> time annihilates space
>
> jobbers thoughts press
> lobes I've always
> valves wavered lost
> parasite pure person
>
> federal pattern of
> feral worker free
> family the state
> that is whose (53)

The piece continues for a further fifty-four, four-line stanzas of a similar content (53-62). The extent to which reading these lines forces a reader—other than one perusing this poem as an educational chore—to do anything, a reader may judge for herself or himself.

The concept that reading something automatically induces a change in the reader desired by the author is flawed not only from a cognitive science perspective but also from a political perspective. Using literary revelations of poverty's effects on people as an example, the critic Eric Schocket points out that:

> [t]hough one might assume that a textual unveiling of poverty would prompt the reader to repudiation and action, such a result is neither necessary nor necessarily efficacious. There is no requisite link between epistemological realism (which claims to know a poverty heretofore hidden from

> view) and political radicalism (which takes actions against economic systems of exploitation). The presumption of just such a link (as in the assertion "If they only knew …") is purely idealist. It is idealist in the simple sense that it takes at face value an implied state of previous innocence that is hardly tenable given the broad tradition of unveiling. (19)

The presumed link between reading and action is also idealist in a more complex sense, Schocket states, in that those who claim such a link are failing to understand the nature of reality. "[T]hose who seek to renounce exploitation simply by representing it fail to recognize the fundamental discontinuity between the real and various attempts to represent it" (19). Schocket feels that a class bias underlies this confusion, and that unless the workings of class considered as a process "shaping cultural frames of reference" are understood, "our political agency will be delimited to pluralistic celebrations or ex post facto denunciations."

Meantime, two different educational ventures have adopted as a corporate slogan this notion of coerced intellectualism. For years, the University of Calgary Press' logo used the tag "Making you think," while the logo tag of TVO (Ontario's public television network) was "Makes you think."

- **Postmodern writing is sophisticated and is an artistic reflection of how language functions.**

Anyone who has taught postsecondary introductory creative writing has encountered students who do not seek to improve their writing by paying close attention to craft, and thus engage in rewriting. Instead, such a student simply wishes her or his genius to be celebrated. These novice writers reject the idea of substitution or elimination of certain nouns, verbs, or modifiers, or deleting or rearranging passages, in order to generate a more effective communication of her or his intended subject matter. Students with this attitude, who mostly quickly drop the course, are extremely defensive about their work. Where confusion regarding their intent due to their lack of craft is pointed out, such students will invariably reply: "My writing can mean whatever the reader wants it to mean." If one mentions that this statement is not true—the piece is not about hunting whales, for instance—their response is to sullenly insist that they are absolutely fine with a reader drawing whatever meaning he or she wants from what they have written.

Similarly, an interpretive problem caused by poor word choice, grammar error, change of tense, inconsistent characterization, and the like, is met with the statement, 'I meant that," apparently indicating that the creation of such confusion is deliberate. Whatever the student's original impulse to communicate a specific feeling, idea, or incident presumably meaningful to the student, he or she is willing to abandon that communication rather than have to work to improve the poem or sample of prose—"improve" in the sense that readers would be able to more easily and deeply perceive what the piece aims to convey.

In an identical manner, postmodern authors protect themselves from any weighing of their mastery—or lack thereof—of the craft of writing. Postmodern literature, as mentioned above, is in essence conceptual art: what is vital is the *idea* behind the form the writing has taken, and not the craft employed in executing this idea. Consider again the creative examples given above, whether Mark Wallace's

> Won't have to testify about
> pigs guilty on the rotunda. Get packing
> nomad street misunderstanding

or Jeff Derksen's

> perceived accepted suffered
> merely naturally unites
> veils cultures call time annihilates space

In neither case can one suggest, as one might in accessible writing, alternative word choice, for example: why is "nomad" a suitable adjective for street? Can one really "pack" a misunderstanding? Two lines both ending in "ing" create a chime for no apparent reason:

isn't this aural effect distracting (the effect is not used in subsequent stanzas)? In addition, is "veils" meant to be a noun or verb? Isn't "time annihilates space" a cliché, lowering the energy of the poem's forward motion? Also irrelevant to ask, given that these are conceptual pieces and not intended to be concerned with writing skills per se, is whether either of these poems in its entirety is too long: is the point made early and then repeated and repeated? Equally, one cannot ask whether the mixing of tenses and/or grammatical moods aids or detracts from communicating the poem's message.

What matters in both poems is the concept that motivated the writing, not the writing itself. Similar to the defense offered by our beginning author, the postmodernist response to any possible critique at the level of craft is that if something doesn't work artistically, then such a shortcoming is part of the writer's *intent* to "trouble," "subvert," "destabilize," "defamiliarize" language. In short, the author is entirely defended.

As I observe elsewhere regarding postmodern writing:

> What is important is the *concept* that lies behind the writing—hence the frequent need for an exhaustive prose exegesis for the art to be understood. ... What is going on in conceptual poetry, including the principles of composition, the content, and much more, is not immediately apparent to a reader, other than a friend or student of the poet. ... Generally, the more opaque the concept—that is, the more that apparent gibberish is revealed to have a method behind it—the more the writing is to be lauded. The cleverness of the concept is vastly more important than the content too: we are asked to admire the genius of the artist in determining the concept rather than being asked to critique the (often banal) content revealed once the clues necessary for understanding the conceptual piece are disclosed in some manner. In short, in a conceptual piece the author hides herself or himself from critique either of diction, form or content. These latter are the very grounds on which mainstream poets are scorned by their "postmodern" colleagues. (117)

Conceptual writing finds a counterpart in conceptual fine art installations, where incomprehensible and/or often crudely executed objects (sometimes in various mediums concurrently displayed) are supposedly justified by the artist's statement that accompanies the exhibit. The statement, if not rendered impenetrable by the use of jargon, reveals the artist's concept—"explains" how the sculptural or found pieces, wall paintings and/or videos demonstrate an idea. Critiquing the choice of, or craft involved in creating or presenting, the objects constituting the exhibit is pointless since what is expected is praise for a tangible gesture toward illustrating a concept.

Conceptual art—written or otherwise—is defended art in another sense besides the barrier its practitioners erect against critique at the level of craft. As the adjective implies, conceptual art is head work; it does not proceed from the heart. Ideas, not emotions, are the content meant to be conveyed. At best, irony substitutes for a broad spectrum of human feelings, from disgust to joy. Compared to the wide range of emotions found in narrative, lyric, or anecdotal verse, postmodern poetry is uniformly flat with regard to feelings: an emotionally detached cognition is all its practitioners allow themselves, and hence allow to their readers. Postmodern writing takes no emotional risks: whatever peaks and valleys of feeling its authors may experience, the relentlessly cerebral tone of their literary productions reveals how these authors hide their emotions from critique.

Robert von Hallberg mentions, in his discussion of postmodern writing referred to earlier, that adherents frequently defend such literature by making the identical claim our neophyte author does: that what is written can mean anything the reader interprets it to mean. For postmodernists, this claim arises from the seminal 1968 essay by Roland Barthes, "The Death of the Author." M.H. Abrams explains that what Barthes, and Michel Foucault (the latter in his essay "What is an Author," 1969), deny is

> the validity of the "function" or "role" hitherto assigned
> in Western discourse to a uniquely individual and purpo-
> sive author, who is conceived … as the initiator, purposive

> planner and (by his or her intentions) the determiner of the form and meanings of a text. ... Instead, the human agent is said to be a disunified subject that is the product of diverse psychosexual conditions, and subjected to the uncontrollable workings of unconscious compulsions. (249).

With the author as a conscious creator out of the way, Abrams notes, the reader is the only one who matters in determining what meaning is communicated by an example of writing. "In the representation of Roland Barthes, the 'death' of the author frees the reader to enter the literary text in whatever way he or she chooses, and the intensity of pleasure yielded by the text becomes proportionate to the reader's abandonment of limits on its signifying possibilities" (250).

This perspective is our beginning writer's dream: if a written work is bad, the fault lies with the reader, not the writer. The author is perfectly insulated from critique. Any perceived shortcomings in technique speak to a lack of reading or interpretive skills in the reader, not to any imperfection in the author's creative abilities. How this stance trickles down to students might be shown by the following sentence in an answer on a 2007 PhD candidacy exam: "Parataxis makes demands of me as a reader to acknowledge that I bring meaning to the poem through my reading, rather than expecting the poem to deliver the meaning to me by following expected conventions."[2] The author is absolved of all responsibilities to use words to communicate—if the reader cannot perceive meaning in what the author has written, or fails to enjoy or otherwise respond to the written text, then the *reader* has not brought enough intelligence to the poem. How sweet this arrangement is for any author.

Clearly, far from producing sophisticated literature, postmodernist authors embody the desire of the most defended of *unskilled* writers: not to be held accountable for the quality of their writing, or for a

---

2 For privacy reasons, the name of the student is not given; candidacy exam document in author's possession.

reader's reaction to the writing. The writing is without flaw simply because the author has written it: any failings lie with those who read the writing.

Evidence of the lack of sophistication of such work might also include the absence, after more than forty years of postmodernism, of a defining creative achievement of postmodern writing. That is, although certain essays — such as Barthes' on the death of the author — can be pointed to as a crowning accomplishment of this *critical* approach, no single literary work is uniformly referenced as a significant creative example of postmodern writing. By contrast, if one accepts that high modernism begins after World War I, a series of recognized exemplary texts appeared within the first seven years of that literary movement. A single year, 1922, saw the publication of "such monuments of modernist innovation as James Joyce's *Ulysses*, T.S. Eliot's *The Waste Land*, and Virginia Woolf's *Jacob's Room*" (Abrams 175). And Ezra Pound published the first sixteen parts of his epic *The Cantos* in 1925 (as *A Draft of XVI Cantos*); Canto 1 had been published in *Poetry* magazine in 1917 (Poetry, "Pound"). The failure of postmodernism to produce a widely acknowledged representative masterpiece or masterpieces underscores the shakiness of the critical approach's claim to either literary (as opposed to critical) significance or status as a literary successor to modernism.

Part of the reason for this failure may be the gap between certain beliefs of postmodernism's adherents and how reality functions, combined with the extremely adversarial nature of the postmodernist milieu. Students (the next generation of professors) pick up the view that language restricts thought, that grammar is an extension of patriarchal, capitalistic, imperialistic oppression, and that pre-postmodern literature is naïve, simplistic, one-dimensional, and its authors and critics dupes of the power relations of their eras. Moreover, postmodern literature is free from political taint, and its authors and critics alone are able to comprehend and navigate moral and social ambiguities and complexities. A postmodern literary critic's task is to denounce the conscious or unconscious complicity with oppression of earlier literature and its authors, and to extol the genius of postmodern texts that only a theoretically informed reader need approach. "The assertion that all poetry must be accessible reinforces patriarchal, capitalist, normative modes of thought in an art that often attempts to subvert these," wrote a student in a 2008 graduate seminar essay. "The type of poetry that is accessible conforms to capitalistic ideals of purposeful diction that can be exchanged for something."[3]

Postmodernist declarations about how language and human perception function have been exhaustively disproved by researchers such as Harvard psychology professor Steven Pinker, formerly director of the Massachusetts Institute of Technology's Center for Cognitive Neuroscience. In a series of books he details the science that shows why postmodernist beliefs about language and the mind are untrue. For instance, far from grammar rules being an oppressive warping of language at the behest of capitalists (specifically, capitalist men), Pinker outlined twenty years ago the research that demonstrates humans are hardwired for rule-based grammar. Among these studies are ones that detail how the children of adult pidgin-speaking Hawaiian field workers, as well as deaf children who were the second generation of sign-language users in Nicaragua, constructed elaborate grammars that enabled the crude languages the youngsters inherited to become enormously more expressive, subtle, and effective as communication (*Language* 33-37).

Pinker discusses the research that debunks "the famous [Edward] Sapir-[Benjamin Lee] Whorf hypothesis of linguistic determinism, stating that people's thoughts are determined by the categories made available by their language, and its weaker version, linguistic relativity, stating that differences among languages cause differences in the thoughts of their speakers" (*Language* 57). Introducing the science that shows why Sapir-Whorf is wrong, Pinker states:

---

3 For privacy reasons, the name of the student is not given; essay document in author's possession.

The idea that thought is the same thing as language is an example of what can be called a conventional absurdity: a statement that goes against all common sense but that everyone believes because they dimly recall having heard it somewhere and because it is so pregnant with implications. ... We have all had the experience of uttering or writing a sentence, then stopping and realizing that it wasn't exactly what we meant to say. To have that feeling, there has to be a "what we meant to say" that is different from what we said. Sometimes it is not easy to find *any* words that properly convey a thought. When we hear or read, we usually remember the gist, not the exact words, so there has to be such a thing as a gist that is not the same as a bunch of words. And if thoughts depended on words, how could a new word ever be coined? (*Language* 57-58)

After a detailed examination of how syntax works, Pinker concludes:

Syntax is complex, but the complexity is there for a reason. For our thoughts are surely even more complex, and we are limited by a mouth that can pronounce a single word at a time. ...

Grammar offers a clear refutation of the empiricist doctrine that there is nothing in the mind that was not first in the senses. ... Though psychologists under the influence of empiricism often suggest that grammar mirrors commands to the speech muscles, melodies in speech sounds, or mental scripts for the ways that people and things tend to interact, I think all these suggestions miss the mark. Grammar is a protocol that has to interconnect the ear, the mouth, and the mind, three very different kinds of machine. It cannot be tailored to any of them but must have an abstract logic of its own.

The idea that the human mind is designed to use abstract variables and data structures used to be ... a shocking and revolutionary claim, because the structures have no direct counterpart in the child's experience. Some of the organization of grammar would have to be there from the start, part of the language-learning mechanism that allows children to make sense out of the noises they hear from their parents. The details of syntax have figured prominently in the history of psychology, because they are a case where complexity in the mind is not caused by learning; learning is caused by complexity in the mind. (*Language* 124-125)

Considering postmodernist notions about language, Pinker says:

The writings of oracles like Jacques Derrida are studded with such aphorisms as "No escape from language is possible," "Text is self-referential," "Language is power," and "There is nothing outside the text." Similarly, [University of California, Irvine professor and former president of the Modern Languages Association] J. Hillis Miller wrote that "language is not an instrument or tool in man's hands, a submissive means of thinking. Language rather thinks man and his 'world' ... if he will allow it to do so." (*Blank Slate* 208)

Pinker notes that some of these claims about language arose because, in a dictionary, words are defined by other words. The deconstructionists consequently argue, Pinker says, that "language is a self-contained system in which words have no necessary connection to reality." And this belief that "language is an arbitrary instrument, not a medium for communicating thoughts or describing reality" leads postmodernists to a number of demonstrably false conclusions about language's properties and uses. "Like all conspiracy theories," Pinker says, "the idea that language is a prisonhouse denigrates its subject by overestimating its power." He calls language "the magnificent faculty that we use to get thoughts from one head to another," a process that can involve numerous methodologies. But language "is not the same as thought, not the only thing that separates humans from other animals, not the basis of all culture, and not an inescapable prisonhouse, an obligatory agreement, the limits of our world, or the determiner of what is imaginable" (*Blank Slate* 208).

Pinker's books discuss these "not"s by describing the science that probed and disproves such claims. Pinker also shows how the post-modernist art world's confusion between *images* and thought, like the literary world's confusion between words and thought, has produced deleterious effects (*Blank Slate* 213-218). He quotes art critic Adam Gopnik ("whose mother and sister are cognitive scientists"): "The view that visual clichés shape beliefs is both too pessimistic, in that it supposes that people are helplessly imprisoned by received stereotypes, and too optimistic, in that it supposes that if you could change the images you could change the beliefs" (*Blank Slate* 217).

The theory of perception that both modernism and postmodernism endorse was long ago bypassed by studies of how the sense organs and the brain function, Pinker states (*Blank Slate* 412).

> When we perceive the products of other people's behaviour, we evaluate them through our intuitive psychology, our theory of mind. We do not take a stretch of language or an artifact like a product or work of art at face value, but try to guess why the producers came out with them and what effect they hope to have on us (as we saw in Chapter 12). Of course, people can be taken in by a clever liar, but they are not trapped in a false world of words and images and in need of rescue by postmodernist artists. (*Blank Slate* 412)

In concluding his assessment of postmodernism, Pinker outlines why cognitive science and cognitive neuroscience are "indispensable to the arts and humanities for at least two reasons." The first is that "the real medium of artists, whatever their genre, is human mental representations" (*Blank Slate* 417). The words, paint, sounds, and so on that any artist employs cannot affect the brain unimpeded. Rather, their effect depends on "a cascade of neural events that begin with the sense organs and culminate in thoughts, emotions, and memories." Research into vision, acoustics, linguistics, mental imagery, and intuitive psychology can illuminate how art tangibly impacts people. "And evolutionary aesthetics can help explain the feelings of beauty and pleasure that can accompany all of these acts of perception" (*Blank Slate* 417). The second reason why science, and not postmodernism's anti-science attitude, is vital to understanding the arts arises because the attraction of art "is not just the sensory experience of the medium but its emotional content and insight into the human condition" (*Blank Slate* 418). And the various aspects of "the timeless tragedies of our biological predicament" that in total constitute the human condition are, as Pinker observes, the manifold "topics of the sciences of human nature."

- **Ezra Pound's dictum "Make it new" refers to the need to craft new forms for writing, and justifies such formal developments.**

Postmodernism's defects consist not only of misapplied descriptors for paratactic writing, unsubstantiated claims of forced cognition, an artistic practice that embraces an unsophisticated novice's highly defended stance, and assertions about language and perception that science has shown are false. Weirdly, for adherents of a critical mindset that positions itself as antithetical to capitalism, a catch-phrase propounded by a Fascist aesthetician is repeatedly invoked in essays, theses and critical articles: Ezra Pound's dictum "Make it new."

Louis Menand, winner of the 2002 Pulitzer Prize in history, in detailing Pound's commitment to Fascism,[4] concludes that Pound's

---

4 Menand dates Pound's increased attraction to anti-Semitism to his interest in Social Credit beginning about 1920 (124). In 1927 Pound met the founder and leader of Fascism, Benito Mussolini, and "came up with the idea of enlisting Mussolini as a patron of the avant-garde. ... Pound concluded that Mussolini had an intuitive grasp of the significance of his poetry" (124). *Making It New*, Pound's book of essays, was published in 1934 (Poetry, "Pound"). "In 1941," Menand writes, "Pound began delivering broadcasts from the Rome studios of Ente Italiana Audizione Radio, attacking the Jews, [then-U.S. President F.D.] Roosevelt, and American intervention in the war" (124). In 1945, Pound was charged with treason, and imprisoned by the American army. Thanks to lobbying by friends, Pound was never tried but confined in a Washington, D.C. mental hospital until 1958, when he returned to Italy. "When he walked off the boat, in Naples," Menand notes, "he gave the Fascist salute" (124).

politics permeate his literary work. "Italian Fascism is integral to 'The Cantos,'" Menand asserts. Two cantos that were for many years left out of the New Directions "complete" edition specifically laud Fascist ideology (124). The section of the poem called "The Pisan Cantos"—published as a book in 1948 and awarded the 1949 Bollingen Prize for Poetry (Poetry, "Pound")—"is, formally, an elegy occasioned by the death of Mussolini at the hands of Italian partisans" (124). Menand quotes a section in which the poet "may sound repentant, but it is not the poet speaking to himself in the second person. The lines are addressed to the American Army ('Half black half white'): the prisoner is raging against his captors. Pound laments, but he does not regret. 'The Pisan Cantos' is a Fascist poem without apologies" (124-125).

Conservatism and anti-Semitism are a central aspect of modernism,[5] despite the writers' and painters' willingness to stretch artistic forms in previously uncommon directions. Perhaps this is why postmodernism's adherents continually quote a Fascist poet by way of authorizing their choices of form. Still, as Menand observes, although several modernist writers were reactionaries "very few" except Pound "were actually Fascists" (124).

And yet Pound's prescription "Make it new" is relentlessly referenced as support for compositional choices made by whoever has invoked the phrase. For instance, the poetry submission information for the (now defunct) *Vancouver Review* cultural journal (which flourished in the opening decade of the 2000s) states:

> *VR* publishes one poem per issue. The subject should be local, in that it relates to BC or Vancouver in some way. "Make it

---

5 T.S. Eliot famously summed up his outlook in 1928 as "classicist in literature, royalist in politics, and Anglo-Catholic in religion" (Stallworthy 2289). Poems of his such as "Gerontion" (1920) and "Burbank with a Baedeker: Bleistein with a Cigar" (also 1920) are unabashedly anti-Semitic. W.B. Yeats, like Eliot a friend of Pound, wrote marching songs for the Irish Fascist group, the Blueshirts (Allison 8). In the fine arts, critic Peter Schjeldahl notes that "the godhead of modernism," Paul Cézanne, "though not an outspoken anti-Semite like [Edgar] Degas and [Auguste] Renoir, sided against the supporters of the [Jewish] Army officer Alfred Dreyfus, who had been falsely convicted of treason" (78).

new" was the credo of Ezra Pound, a poet often credited with ushering in 20th-century poetry that shelved Victorian artifice and sentimentality in favour of diamond-sharp imagery and harder truths. It doubles as *VR*'s call to poets to help us revision this part of the world. (*Vancouver*)

Presumably those "harder truths" that Pound ushered in do not include the poet's "attacks on ... Jews as moneylenders and financiers of wars, a classic type of anti-Semitism" (Menand 124). How much easier to pretend that Pound had two brains: a Fascist brain which can be safely ignored, and a different brain he inserted when he wrote poems and important critical pronouncements.

But what does Pound's pronouncement mean? In critical essays, articles or theses at any level, most who refer to the injunction appear to believe the pronoun "it" refers to "literary form" or "critical concept." William Wenthe observes, however, that

> [p]ersons who repeat that phrase as an insipid slogan of the avant-garde think that the "it" refers to some broad abstraction like "art" or "culture." But for Pound, who knowingly quotes the phrase from a Chinese emperor of the 18th century BCE ..., the "it" refers to the concrete and familiar, refreshed by daily attention (the emperor wrote the phrase on his bathtub). (34-35)

In short, the phrase has to do with perceiving the ordinary world with a freshness, an intensity—the latter qualities being an achievement of all good writing. The directive has *nothing* to do with paratactic form or any of the other postmodernist ends the "it" is variously conscripted into representing.

But even if the phrase *was* a clarion call to write paratactic or other formally unusual verse, why would a Fascist sympathizer issue such a call? That is, how might Fascism benefit from Pound's stance? More accurately, how might the phrase as Pound *intended* it to mean relate to the goals of Fascism? Is something that is "new" automatically improved, better for people, as in the "new and improved" succession of products that capitalism has found necessary to promote in order to ensure continuing profits?

The ideology of Fascism, like its German counterpart, National Socialism, depended on a falsification or obscuring of the past in order to justify the "new" authoritarian state and its economic and social order. Today we see globalized corporate capitalism wholeheartedly espouse the "Make it new" doctrine via planned obsolescence, the promotion of previously unknown anxieties for purposes of increasing sales ("ring around the collar" being the classic), the introduction of incompletely tested defective products (Thalidomide, or Microsoft's succession of Windows programs), the never-ending stream of the latest "must have" luxury goods and services, etc. The falsification or obscuring of the past, in order to replace history's specific achievements and understandings with the "new," has its counterpart in postmodernism's attacks on and/or rejection of the literary canon. Who benefits socially and economically when a community or a nation's literary past is disparaged, expunged or rewritten?

IV

Given postmodernism's evident usefulness to reactionaries of many stripes, and given its internal flaws and contradictions, what is its likely future? Certainly once it passes out of academic fashion it will have an afterlife, in the way scholars trained to venerate the critical precepts of T.S. Eliot continued to teach and publish from that perspective for decades after his ideas were superseded as a primary font of critical ideas.[6] Conceptual art, including paratactic poetry, will continue to

---

6 A graduate student in literature today, scanning through Derrida's prose to find the perfect quotation to bolster a paper the student is writing and to thus please her or his instructor, would likely be astonished to learn of the former veneration of Eliot's critical acumen. The Poetry Foundation's summation of Eliot's career quotes U.S. poet Delmore Schwartz, writing in the *Partisan Review* in 1949: "When we think of the character of literary dictators

be produced, even if its academic status wanes. Poet, psychologist and California State University, Long Beach, professor Charles Harper Webb sees the production of such art as a tiny subset of Darwinian fitness indicators: "By evolving to favour fitness indicators, members of a species favour mates most likely to produce viable offspring" (60). Webb quotes evolutionary psychologist Geoffrey Miller as believing that artists, conceptual and otherwise, display their fitness to reproduce "by making something that lower-fitness competitors could not make" (60). And such indicators apply to consumers of art as well:

> The ability to understand good poetry constitutes … a fitness-indicator *for the reader*, showing that he/she can perform the required mental feats, as well as keep up with the poet's (presumably first-rate) mind.
> Such displays of mental fitness increase the reader's sense of status, self-esteem and overall desirability. (60)

However, the bad news for postmodernists is that Miller believes that a poem fails as a fitness display unless the work strikes a balance between being too obviously comprehensible and too hard to grasp. "If the poem is too difficult to understand, readers can't judge the poet's fitness, and may lose self-esteem in the process. They feel stupid, dense, insensitive, out of the cultural loop—anything but intellectually fit. Even when readers know the writer is at fault, they feel frustrated and annoyed" (61).

Of course, as long as postmodernism is regarded as a valid critical pursuit, and in some professors' and academic programs' eyes as the dominant one, some students will take advantage of this to engage in

---

in the past, it is easy to see that since 1922, at least, Eliot has occupied a position in the English-speaking world analogous to that occupied by Ben Jonson, Dryden, Pope, Samuel Johnson, Coleridge and Matthew Arnold" (Poetry, "Eliot"). Writing in 1956, Rene Wellek, a founder of comparative literature studies and a historian of culture, concluded: "T.S. Eliot is by far the most important critic of the twentieth century in the English-speaking world" (Poetry, "Eliot").

fitness display. "I watched a student writer transform himself," Webb says, "from a plain-spoken neo-Bukowski [maverick U.S. author Charles Bukowski (1920-1994)] to a cryptologist-in-verse, blatantly seeking to carve a niche for himself in my class, and increase his cachet with female students. His strategy worked, too!" (66)

Yet Webb sees a difficulty with using postmodern art to demonstrate evolutionary fitness:

> Because some modern poems are difficult works of genius, some poets write difficult poems in hopes that they'll be works of genius too. But the poem that withholds too much in order to protect the poet's ego and/or to appear impressive and "deep," is not just difficult; it's as poorly made as (and may be synonymous with) the poem with garbled syntax, inept pacing, wavering tone, botched imagery. ... "Experimental" poems may intentionally thwart reader expectations for such qualities as closure, emotional engagement, and identifiable meaning. The theory behind such strategies ... gives rise to poems that are self-consciously, proudly, and impenetrably difficult. Poems arising from these strategies use extreme withholding—discontinuity, opacity, indeterminate syntax and diction, and whatever else they can do—to confound and shift reader expectations. (62).

The problem arises, claims Webb, because as long as postmodernism basks in academic approbation, postmodernists' fitness displays are those of an elite. Such displays may successfully function for a time, but their legitimacy must be questioned (62). "How do we account for the professional success of poets who actively strive for obliquity, opacity, indeterminacy, and in some cases, boring monotony, and whose own work bears out their assumption that meaning does not exist" (62-63)?

He quotes Miller as stating that "elite aesthetics concerns the objects of art that highly educated, rich elites learn are considered worthy of comment by their peers" (63). Whereas regular aesthetics focus on craft, elite aesthetics focus on "the viewer's response as a social display" (63). Elites "often try to distinguish themselves from the common run of humanity by replacing natural human tastes … with artfully contrived preferences … [by which they] can display their intelligence, learning ability, and sensitivity to emerging cultural norms." Such a fitness indicator is based on social *status*, however, rather than artistic achievement, according to Webb. "The preference for extremely difficult poetry may enhance the status and self-esteem of the elite; but, like bound feet, elite aesthetics encourage poems to develop in grotesque ways, leading to the literary equivalent of a whole court hobbling because the queen is lame" (63).

Webb acknowledges that given the spectrum of human taste, some individuals will savour writing or reading extremely inaccessible poems. Such an activity, though, is bound up with a dubious morality.

> [T]he difficulty of telling bad-difficult from good-difficult advances the strategy of the elite, inadvertent and unconscious though that strategy may be.
> "Most people want to be able to interpret works of art as indicators of the artist's style and creativity," Miller states. "Certain styles of art make this difficult to do." Most readers must either reject these styles, or rely on the judgment of critics and professors: the elite. (63)

The latter choice is spelled out by Webb:

> [M]any readers … can't tell the difference between difficult good and difficult bad poems. Here the Emperor's New Clothes Syndrome comes into play:
> Poet A wins the Formidable Prize. Reader Z can't understand A's poems and doesn't like them. However, Z recognizes and applauds the many competing aesthetics in American poetry, and does not wish to appear narrow-minded, intolerant, judgmental, or dense. And what

is Z's judgment worth, compared to that of the Judges who chose A, and have won Formidable Prizes themselves? Fearing to reveal incompetence as a reader, Z casts his lot with the experts, convinces himself that he loves A's book, and feels a lot better about himself. (64)

So paratactic poetry will continue to be written, whatever the future of the postmodern aesthetic, even if such poetry overall "makes a poor fitness indicator, since its success as poetry is so difficult to judge" (64). Advantages for the writer remain, if not evolutionary ones. As Webb notes: "Difficulty erects a screen between writer and audience, protecting the writer from self-revelation, and deflecting criticism. Incomprehensibility may confer invulnerability" (63).

As well, there are non-evolutionary advantages for a consumer of postmodern art, even though, as Webb remarks, "[f]or all the theorists' talk of training a new kind of reader, few have emerged" (65) in the past four decades. Postmodern art offers its audience a chance to engage in one-upmanship. "[A]s Adam Gopnik has pointed out, the political messages of most postmodernist pieces are utterly banal, like 'racism is bad[,]' [b]ut they are stated so obliquely that viewers are made to feel morally superior for being able to figure them out" (*Blank Slate* 416).

Yet the continued existence of the postmodernist mind-set offers a more malevolent potential than the small pleasures of vanity that a sense of moral superiority provides. In the struggle to oppose those practices of corporations willing in the name of maximizing profits to sacrifice the ability of the biosphere to sustain human existence, literature—literary nonfiction, and, yes, even poetry—has been playing a role. We can currently observe literary postmodernism's adherents being mustered to try to derail this struggle, to quieten literature's involvement in the fight against the causes of climate change, even as postmodernist ideas helped quiet social activism among college and university students. The anti-science attitudes promulgated by the postmodernist mind-set, along with the effort to ensure postsecondary students and graduates cannot effectively communicate to ordinary citizens, are a help with this latest reactionary project.

An overview of approaches to ecopoetics in a recent essay by Maine poet Arielle Greenberg illustrates the postmodernist strategy to shift writers' and readers' focus away from a clear expression of love of the earth—surely the only sustainable means to endure the long-drawn-out combat that will be required to end globalized capitalism's despoiling of our planet. Greenberg quotes approvingly a 2011 list attempting a definition of ecopoetics prepared by Jonathan Skinner, founder of the journal *ecopoetics*. Besides the expected constituents of the field, such as "poetry of wilderness and deep ecology," we are told that for some readers

> ecopoetics is not a matter of theme, but of how certain poetic methods model ecological processes like complexity, non-linearity, feedback loops, and recycling. ... Or how poetic experimentation complements scientific methods in extending a more reciprocal relation to alterity [jargon for "a difference from a worldview or state of existence considered to be the norm"]. ... Or even how translation can diversify the "monocrop" of a hegemonic [jargon for "predominant"] language like English. (27)

Greenberg's essay goes on to feature poems incorporating "ideas and strategies ... refusing, rebutting or subverting some of the traditional or historic modes of writing about our habitats" (27). Thus nonlinear writing of any kind, along with "experimental" poetry on any subject, plus poems that intend to attack the canon of nature writing, and even translation on any subject all can qualify—through the magic of postmodern theory—as ecological.

How this plays out in more concrete terms might be demonstrated in a recent graduate English program application. The student applying for admission was proposing to extend [Mark] Wallace's definition [of "postlanguage" poets, that is, postmodernist poets coming after the original Language poets (Mukherjee)] to five Canadian poets — Erin Mouré, Christopher Dewdney, Lisa Robertson, Fred Wah and Dennis Lee[7]— showing how their work suggests positive ways of speaking about nature, by enacting the inextricable relationship of nature and language.

Needless to say, the proposed discovery of a link between nature and language would not involve a scientific approach. "My dissertation will also deprivilege lyric poetry as the dominant vehicle of ecopoetics." A supporting statement from a junior faculty member[8] at the student's current institution assured adjudicators of the application that the student's "project promises to contribute to the task of defining which bodies of Canadian Literature stand to be studied in relation to the environment, disrupting the assumption that it is self-evidently those in which nature figures at the level of content."

Eliminating a consideration of nature from the content of writing intended to oppose governments and corporations for not enacting measures designed to minimize or reverse the degradation of the biosphere is just one of the ways the postmodernist ethic can help protect the status quo.[9] In addition, the social restructuring necessary to tackle

---

7 Mouré and Robertson are full-fledged postmodernist writers; the other three write in varying degrees of inaccessibility.

8 For privacy reasons, the names of the student and the faculty member are not given.

9 An awareness that literary postmodernism poses a threat to an ecological awareness, despite the critical approach's claims to the contrary, is not a new idea. D.M.R. Bentley, of the University of Western Ontario, noted in a 1990 essay that "insofar as certain strains of critical theory have stressed the importance of language to the exclusion or near-exclusion of other matters, they have done literature a disservice by placing it in a realm remote from its physical, emotional, and moral contexts" (88). Bentley notes that poems cannot be divorced from the physical. "The eye that reads, the voice that speaks, the ear that hears, the brain that perceives, comprehends, interprets, and remembers: all are physical, as, of course, are books, and pages, and print." He argues that a truly "ecological approach to Canadian poetry offers resistance to any and all forces that participate or cooperate in disprizing environments, people, and poems of their diversity by threatening to obliterate their unique, local, regional, and national characteristics" (87). Observing that "what is at stake is nothing less than the

climate change must be argued for in a milieu of spin, "expert" jargon, advertising, propaganda, social distraction (celebrity journalism and government-funded spectacles such as the Olympics or foreign wars) and outright lying by authorities. Postmodernism's vaunted ambiguity and lack of closure, along with its abandonment of linear narrative structure and clear referentiality, fit in well with globalism's insistence that any narrative of its impairment of the quality of daily life must be blurred or otherwise obscured. Postmodernism's adherents thus by default assist globalization to convince the public that there's no such thing as societal values or societal well-being except as transnational commercial enterprises define them (unambiguously, repeatedly and resoundingly).

The twenty-first century so far is off to a start as horrendous and murderous as the twentieth: continual wars, fanatical ideologies, imperialism (albeit now under a trademark as often as under a flag), extremes of wealth and poverty. If climate change is factored into the analysis, perhaps the current century is off to a worse start than the previous one. The set of ideas and derivative artistic creations that constitute postmodernism is, for reasons discussed above, not likely to help achieve a happier, more democratic personal and collective existence for human beings, nor to end the transformation of the biosphere.

Art ultimately is self-expression, and the politics of narrowing access to producing and comprehending academically approved acts of self-expression to a small, specially trained cohort does no credit to the artists or cheerleaders of this development. Lauding as "innovative" artists who take academically pre-approved "risks" in their compositional strategies is a minor part of the debasement of language that is postmodernism in practice. In our era the ability of political and economic power structures to employ words to mislead, confuse and ultimately oppress citizens has been vastly increased by a century of

survival of terrestrial life," he concludes that "an ecological poetics is opposed to any system, be it multinational capitalism, architectural postmodernism, or deconstruction, insofar as that system contributes to the homogenization of nature and its creations, be they physical or linguistic." Bentley is aware of modernism's failure as well to adopt an ecological outlook (89); he calls for ecological writing that is not postmodern but "past-modern"(103).

trial, error, and advances in understanding how the mind and emotions function. Surely what would be beneficial to our communities would be an academic movement promoting clarity of expression along with critical thinking about how words can so effectively manipulate people to their detriment—critical thinking that incorporates the relevant scientific discoveries.

In terms of literary studies, we can do better than to promote a mindset bristling with negative rectitude, one that encourages contempt for the literary achievements of the past and for the majority of contemporary authors, while lavishing unqualified praise on the few writers producing "theory-based" literature. Which adherents of postmodernism express *delight* in reading literature? And yet, likely this joy in the written word was what brought them into English studies, or creative writing, in the first place. Regarding as the only worthwhile writing that which must be approached as a puzzle to be solved (or which a reader is "forced" to solve), while simultaneously hunting through accessible creative works for a reason to castigate the author, often for the fault of having been born before our enlightened current age, is not a route to encouraging people to discover literature's pleasures and insights.

In this century, perhaps due to the influence of television and the new media so hysterically promoted by the corporations, attention spans are shrinking (Keyes, Liu) along with the capacity to imagine (Bly 186-87; Ouellette), read for enjoyment (Zaki), and empathize with others (Zaki). Given these developments, would preferable literary studies not be ones that entice students to experience the wonders found in reading, to become acquainted with the spectrum of emotions and other vital knowledge imaginative literature can offer—an approach to literature that opens up the world? Would more astute and more up-to-the-minute literary studies not be ones that welcome what the sciences of our age have to teach, rather than reiterating long-ago-disproven pronouncements from certain individuals, bromides without any evidence to support their claims?

Like the surge in fundamentalist religion, in reactionary politics, in assaults on the gains women have achieved during the past half-century, and in acceptance of an ultra-wealthy social class, postmodernism is an understandable reaction to a world that seems to some people to be changing frighteningly fast. But less backward-looking critical stances are needed if the production and study of literature is to help our communities safely navigate this difficult passage in human history.

WORKS CITED

Abrams, M.H. *A Glossary of Literary Terms*. 8th ed. Boston: Thompson Wadsworth, 2005. Print.

Academy of American Poets. "A Brief Guide to Language Poetry." *Academy of American Poets*, 2004. Web. 22 July 2014.

Ahmad, A. Muhammad. "1968-1971: The League of Revolutionary Black Workers." *libcom*, 28 Oct. 2005. Web. 27 June 2014.

Allison, Jonathan. "Introduction: Fascism, Nationalism, Deception." *Yeats' Political Identities: Selected Essays*. Ann Arbor: U of Michigan P, 1996. 1-26. Print.

beaulieu, derek. "Summer Triangle." *Post-Prairie*. Ed. Jon Paul Fiorentino and Robert Kroetsch. Vancouver: Talonbooks, 2005. 15. Print.

Bentley, D.M.R. "'Along the Line of Smoky Hills': Further Steps toward an Ecological Poetics." *Greening the Maple*. Ed. Ella Soper and Nicholas Bradley. Calgary: U of Calgary P, 2013. 85-107. Print.

Betts, Gregory. "Before *Our Time*: Radical English-Canadian Poetries Across the Post/Modern Divide." *Canadian Poetry* 60 (Spring/Summer 2007): 22-45. Print.

Bly, Robert. *The Sibling Society*. New York: Addison-Wesley, 1995. Print.

Breton, André and Diego Rivera. "Manifesto for an Independent Revolutionary Art." *Marxists,* 2001. Web. 31 July 2014.

Buruma, Ian. "Populists Who Speak the (Relative) Truth." *The Globe and Mail*, 12 March 2012. Web. 3 November 2012.

Christakos, Margaret. "Banish." *Event* 42.1 (Spring/Summer 2013): 49. Print.

Collins, Billy. Introduction. *180 More*. New York: Random, 2005. Print.

Derksen, Jeff. *Transnational Muscle Cars*. Vancouver: Talonbooks, 2003. Print.

Fiorentino, Jon Paul and Robert Kroetsch. "Post-Prairie Poetics: A Dialogue." *Post-Prairie*. Ed. Jon Paul Fiorentino and Robert Kroetsch. Vancouver: Talonbooks, 2005. 9- 13. Print.

Foster, Clarise. "An Interview with Rachel Zolf." *Contemporary Verse 2* 34.1 (Summer 2011): 9-23. Print.

Fromm, Harold. "Collecting Science: Sokal, Dawkins, and McKibben." *The Hudson Review* 61.3 (Autumn 2008): 573-579. Print.

Grady, Wayne. *Technology*. Groundwork Guides. Toronto: Groundwood, 2010. Print.

Greenberg, Arielle. "That Greeny Power: Recent Works of Ecopoetics." *The American Poetry Review* 43.4 (July/August 2014): 27-29. Print.

Hayden, Tom. *Writings for a Democratic Society.* San Francisco: City Lights, 2008. Print.

Hunt, Ronald. *Poetry Must Be Made by All! Transform the World!* Catalogue 84. Stockholm: Moderna Museet, 1969. Print.

Keyes, Alexa. "Infographic: The Shrinking Attention Span." *NBC News*, 21 May 2014. Web. 9 Aug. 2014.

Levy, Ariel. "Lift and Separate." *The New Yorker* 85.37 (Nov. 16, 2009): 78-80. Print.

Liu, Ziming. "Reading Behavior in the Digital Environment: Changes in Reading Behavior Over the Past Ten Years." *Journal of Documentation* 61.6 (2005): 700-712. Print.

McLeod, S.A. "Cognitive Dissonance." *Simply Psychology*, 2008. Web. 31 July 2014.

Menand, Louis. "The Pound Error." *The New Yorker* 84.17 (June 9 & 16, 2008): 123-127. Print.

Mendelson, Edward. "'What We Love, Not Are.'" *The New York Review of Books* 55.14 (Sept. 25, 2008): 28-32. Print.

Mukherjee, Aryanil. "Beyond Post Modern Poetry: A Conversation with Mark Wallace." *Karub Online,* 2002. Web. 7 Aug. 2014.

Ouellette, Jeannine. "The Death and Life of American Imagination." *The Rake*, 16 Oct. 2007. Web. 9 Aug. 2014.

Pinker, Steven. *The Blank Slate*. New York: Viking, 2002. Print.

—. *The Language Instinct*. New York: HarperCollins, 1995. Print.

Poetry Foundation. "T.S. Eliot." *Poetry Foundation*, n.d.. Web. 5 Aug. 2014.

—. "Ezra Pound." *Poetry Foundation*, n.d.. Web. 2 Aug. 2014.

Poetzsch, Markus. "Towards an Ethical Literary Criticism: the Lessons of Levinas." *The Antigonish Review* 158 (Summer 2009): 127-134. Print.

Rakita, Gordon F.M. "Strange Anti-Science Bedfellows." *SAS Bulletin* 33.2 (Summer 2010): 25-26. Print.

Ruth, Jennifer. "A Downwardly-Mobile Professor Reads Bruce Robbins' *Upward Mobility and the Common Good*." *Minnesota Review* 70 (Spring/Summer 2008): 167-171. Print.

Schjeldahl, Peter. "Game Change: Cézanne, Card Players and the Birth of Modernism." *The New Yorker* 87.2 (Feb. 28, 2011): 78-79. Print.

Schocket, Eric. *Vanishing Moments: Class and American Literature* (Ann Arbor: U of Michigan P, 2006). Print.

Sim, Stuart and Borin Van Loon. *Introducing Critical Theory*. Duxford: Icon, 2001. Print.

Stafford, William. "An Interview by Thomas E. Kennedy." *The American Poetry Review*. 25.3 (May/June 1996): 49-55. Print.

Stallworthy, John and Jahan Ramazani. *The Norton Anthology of English Literature: The Twentieth Century and After*. 8th Ed. New York: Norton, 2006. Print.

Vancouver Review. "Submissions." *Vancouver Review*, 2010. Web. 6 Dec. 2011.

TMiller and Associates. *Linkedin*. Web. 25 July 2014.

von Hallberg, Robert. "Lyric Thinking." *TriQuarterly* 120 (2005): 171-193. Print.

Wallace, Mark. "Any Publicity is Good Publicity." *The Capilano Review* 3.6 (September 2008): 82. Print.

Wayman, Tom. "Challenges of the Quotidian: Accessibility and the Poetry of Glen Sorestad, Robert Currie, Stephen Scriver and William Robertson." *The Literary History of Saskatchewan*. Vol. 2—Progressions. Ed. David Carpenter. Regina: Coteau, 2014. 112-147. Print.

Webb, Charles Harper. "The Poem as Fitness Display." *The Writer's Chronicle* 40.5 (March/April 2008): 60-66. Print.

Wenthe, William. "The Glamour of Words." *The American Poetry Review*. 42.2 (March-April 2013): 31-35. Print.

Williams, Jeffery J. "A Life in Criticism: An Interview with M.H. Abrams." *The Minnesota Review* 69 (Fall/Winter 2007): 71-93. Print.

Zaki, Jamil. "What, Me Care? Young Are Less Empathetic." *Scientific American*, 23 Dec. 2010. Web. 9 August 2014.

LOVE'S PROVINCES
AND TERRITORIES

I began to assemble *The Dominion of Love* while recuperating from an emotionally painful rejection. All one summer I had courted, but in August she concluded her life's path would be better if it took a different direction than one decided jointly with me.

When a heart's desire of mine is thwarted, I find myself overtaken by flu-like symptoms—searing physical aches, extreme lassitude, a mental and bodily fog which settles heavily over each act of normal life. Such hurt is one of the many provinces and territories of romantic love, along with ecstasy and pleasure.

When I love deeply, I believe I risk no less than myself: I admit to myself and to an important other what I want. Because I exist in an apparently random universe, however, no outcome in my life is certain except growth and decay—in short, change. And change, to me, usually feels as if it is a shift toward the worse, no matter where the change ultimately leads. My love may not be what the beloved requires or wishes; love directed toward me may not be good for me. Yet agony and fear, grief and rage can be my response in the moment to a nudge the universe is giving both of us toward something more satisfying.

Shakespeare's *Twelfth Night* opens with Orsino, the Duke of Illyria, suggesting that music is the food of love. Contemporary behavioural theories, though, propose that love's sustenance is found elsewhere. We are advised that we each emerge from childhood, as well as from teenage or adult experiences, with adopted patterns of response to people close to us and to those who are potentially mates or lovers.

These patterns may enhance or discourage intimacy, self-revelation, kindness—nutrients love needs to grow. Love demands, too, an honest self-awareness, and a willingness to understand as fully as possible the roots and consequences of one's chosen behaviours toward the beloved. Also necessary for love to thrive, according to these theories, are an openness to receive the news about the patterns the beloved employs, plus an ability to alter behaviours perceived as destructive to trust and sharing.

Such a complicated way of viewing love is very different from the vision the Romantic poets at the start of the nineteenth century— Keats, Shelley—sang about. The central characteristic of this literature, emotional effusion (Wordsworth's "spontaneous overflow of powerful feelings"), remains the definition of both love and poetry many people today cling to. But the nineteenth and twentieth century handed society a series of unsettling lessons: the scientific method, Darwin, Marx, Freud, and the women's movement. We became aware of a historiography of our feelings. Our past—social, economic, cultural, personal—very strongly influences our present emotions. The force of our feelings is undisputed; their spontaneity is less certain.

Poets in our era, like everyone else, have to love amid a milieu that instructs us to take an unflinching look at our relations with others. The mystery that is love alters its appearance as we comprehend more—just as every other baffling aspect of our lives changes when we increase our understanding of it. Our species apparently is programmed to be curious. We are compelled to examine each facet of our world, and to develop increasingly complex tools to facilitate this probing.

In the midst of such a process, we are tempted to regard the past as the repository of a surety, a simplicity, we yearn for in an age of ambiguity. But the Romantic era that shapes our most sentimental view of love also gave us Blake, who saw even then that humanity had to move from innocence through experience to a form of existence more self-aware, if less magical. The goal of acquiring this knowledge is not to abandon the awe once provided by myths. The aim is to root wonder amid the actual, the everyday, not to encounter and celebrate it only in the ephemeral or ethereal.

During the past 200 years how we draw the map of love has been transformed as significantly as how we chart the globe or the heavens, or how we describe the sub-atomic universe or the human unconscious. In *The Dominion of Love* the poets of Canada at the start of the Third Millennium sketch our version of love's cartography, geology, geography.

Of course the overall message of the poets here is affected by my intervention as compiler of this anthology. The extent of love's domain is huge, as vast as Canada itself. I have narrowed my choice of landscape to romance; absent are poems of love for children, things, parents, siblings, the dead. I am aware, too, that the body is able to speak as eloquently about love as can the feelings or the mind. Yet for this collection I have selected material on the love/sex continuum closer to the emotions than to the erotic.

Both joy and unhappiness are sources of poetry; on that spectrum I have chosen material nearer to delight than its opposite. But undermining all my discriminations is the supple strength of the art form: poetry rejects any attempt to narrowly categorize it. Love of others besides a mate or spouse surface in these poems, as does a celebration of the marvels of the beloved's body. The agonies, disappointments, betrayals that are also features of love's topography are expressed despite my presiding intent.

The poems of *The Dominion of Love* are, too, poems I admire. My admiration is subjective, based—as are my other decisions that focus this collection—on my exploratory adventures and residence in the dominion, and on my own artistic sensibilities. One literary event from my past that helped craft this anthology is the publication in 1962 of a book of Canadian love poems edited by Irving Layton, *Love Where the Nights Are Long*.

I was a teenager when Layton's volume appeared. I found the collection impressive then, as did the public: in the ensuing decade *Love Where the Nights Are Long* was reprinted four times. As a bow in Layton's direction, and to emphasize that in the arts we all stand on each other's shoulders, I decided *The Dominion of Love* should be precisely the length of Layton's book: 50 poems.

Yet how strange to reread Layton's anthology after three decades, as I did when I started to prepare my collection. The pages of Layton's gathering starkly reveal the extent to which the dominion has changed.

Layton presents 44 love poems by 22 male poets, and 6 poems by 4 female poets. Issues of gender balance aside, I felt this choice does not reflect my own experiences. The women of my acquaintance have pondered and discussed love relationships in much greater detail and much more frequently than the men I know. Indeed, my women friends at times communicate a decided impatience with my and other men's opaqueness when exposed to love. Men to them seem participants in an enterprise who have not bothered to familiarize themselves with the rules, strategy, tactics of the endeavour. This is the identical impatience men traditionally have voiced toward women's requests to engage in formerly male activities such as hunting and some other sports, or the priesthood and various other trades.

My goal for *The Dominion of Love* was to gather 50 excellent English-language Canadian love poems written by 25 women and 25 men. The final result confirms (or was influenced by) my observation above about women paying closer attention to the subject: women outnumber men in my anthology. Yet as a means again to honour precedent, five of the poets here (although not their poems) also are included in Layton's book: Birney, Cogswell, Cohen, Purdy, Waddington.

Like Layton's selection of contributors, his introduction, "What Canadians Don't Know About Love," appears to be a document from a remote past—*our* past, but a generation or two behind us. "Love," Layton trumpets, "works on us the way great poetry does: it transports us out of our habitual selves and allows the angels to sweep new knowledge into the vacated space. When we return we stand higher and better."

Would that were true! How well we understand now that a Nazi concentration camp guard, a South American torturer, a bank executive or a homophobic columnist can fall in love, commence living with the person he or she adores, and yet not quit his or her hideous occupation. Behavioural theorists argue for a continuity in our conduct: we behave fundamentally the same in each part of our lives. Not romance, contemporary wisdom teaches, but self-knowledge will save us. Love—particularly failures at love—may motivate us to embark on a voyage of self-discovery that might ultimately lead us to improve how we function in the world. But love is not the vessel which bears us away.

And Layton, in his eagerness to prove Canadians have a special aptitude for writing love poetry, is quick to disparage poets of other eras and nations. In dismissing the French, he blusters: "What can grocers selling herrings and pepper know about the exaltations of love?" We might as foolishly ask, "What can university teachers of English [as Layton was for much of his working life] know about the exaltations of love?" For love, though it is no guarantee of our good conduct, comes to us all. The intensity of our feelings may be strongly influenced by our occupation—by how our work affects our sense of self-worth, for example, and by the amount of energy and money and opportunity for leisure our employment allows us during our hours *off* the job. But identical tasks can be organized differently on different jobsites, for instance by a union or non-union employer. With few exceptions, we cannot point to certain occupations as inherently destructive of affection. Even soldiers have been known to write good love poetry. A grocery clerk may indeed be a more passionate lover and poet than a university professor.

I believe the poems of *The Dominion of Love* are as fine as any love poetry of our time not because of their authors' nationality or job but because of their authors' emotional and literary skill. The first section here, "You Have the Lovers," groups together poems that to me express the breathless wonder we feel—or at least *I* feel—when the great wave of romantic love breaks over our heads. The second section, "In Darkness We Find Each Other," celebrates the curious fact that love—like a bat—often does best at night. The night is also metaphorical. Perhaps in the absence of the literal or figurative light, we have a greater need for love in our lives: we comprehend its importance to us most powerfully.

The poems of these first two sections represent the kinds of writing I expected to find when I began to assemble *The Dominion of Love.* The third grouping of poems, "Married Love," collects what for me was a surprise—a theme of praise for long-term relationships, of the joy of marriage. Interestingly, this is the only section where the number of poems by men is larger than those by women. The self-help shelves of our bookshops contain a plethora of titles on the subject of Steven Carter and Julia Sokol's 1987 bestseller, *Men Who Can't Love.* Yet clearly there are males who are far from commitment-phobic, who hymn the difficulties and rewards of loving someone over an extended time.

The final section, "Away With Words," groups two poems that explore the tangled links between love and the descriptions of love in words. We frequently turn to words—or to music, or to other arts—to release the sweet pressure love creates in us. But ultimately love is not made on the printed page, but through our actions—our gestures large and small, our establishment of carnal and emotional intimacy, our creation of a joined life. Whether Canadians or not, whether poets or not, lovers announce their desire for a close connection with another person as much with the body as with nouns and verbs, as much with everyday gestures of kindness or thoughtfulness as with the products of pen, keyboard, and printing press. As complex as the written description of anything may be, the state of love is far more intricate and textured and multi-layered. "In love," insists Rhona McAdam in these pages, "we are beasts of infinity": a mix of the animal and the philosophical that has unwaveringly puzzled and thrilled our species.

McAdam characterizes romantic love as "finding a reason to come together / without killing the wildness we each carry // like a gift we haven't decided to share." The poets of *The Dominion of Love* offer to share their gift of a portion of the map of love. Since this is terrain we all reside in, an overview of even a segment of the landscape can be a useful, a treasured, asset. My hope is that the poems of this anthology will help make anyone's journey across these provinces and territories more sure-footed, cheerful, exciting, successful. We are travellers in these regions all our lives. Those who have written about where we journey provide us with the same benefits of any national literature— an expanded sense of place, and a deeper perception of those who inhabit this country.

THE BLOODHOUND
AND THE SKEIN
On Narrative in Poetry

L anguage by nature is narrative. Each verb informs us of the adventures—large or small—that a certain noun of our acquaintance is having. Such pervasive grammatical gossip means that poetry, like every linguistic artifact, is in its essence a story-telling device.

Thus poetry and narrative are joined at the heart from birth. Certain types of poetry—lyric, exhortative, declarative—at times assert the narrative in a below-the-surface statement: *I feel, I urge, I believe.* But *all* words imply a speaker, an "I" who is relating a tale for we the readers/listeners. Any information communicated to us through language imparts a story, if only the origin of the emotions associated with a concept summoned up in the mind by another person's words. Narrative in writing may be explicit, implicit, disguised, or even exiled. But to proffer a phrase or sentence is unfailingly to evoke a tale. Where two or three words are gathered together in language's holy name, there story is in the midst of them.

My life as a writer began with an enjoyment of obvious story in song: the lyrics of campfire tunes and spirituals I sang as a Boy Scout, and the mini-narratives of 1950s popular music ("The Wayward Wind") and rock and roll ("Green Door," "Won't You Wear My Ring?"). Overlapping such tunes was the transformation of folk song into a mainstream commercial enterprise eventually reaching even the town of Prince Rupert on the rainy north coast of B.C. where I entered my adolescence (The Kingston Trio's "Tom Dooley"). Then I was enveloped in the 1960s folk—and folk-rock—explosion: Joan Baez, Tim Hardin, Ian & Sylvia, Fred Neil, Jefferson Airplane. And Bob Dylan. Through the decades, the stories just keep on comin': The Eagles, Paul Simon, Bruce Hornsby, Stan Ridgway, James Keelaghan, John Hiatt.

My first link to contemporary *poetry* was formed of three strands, all overtly narrative, which wound through my love of song. Family was the first of these threads or cords: I grew up in a household where my father was a fan of poetry generally and contemporary Canadian poetry particularly, a rare characteristic for a pulp mill chemist. On our bookshelves were the latest by F.R. Scott, Eli Mandel, Irving Layton, Leonard Cohen, and more. Both my mother and father had been political activists in Toronto in the 1930s, and their left-wing connections were augmented through my mother's trade of social work. Thus from various sources my parents knew Dorothy Livesay and Miriam Waddington and Earle Birney's wife Esther; my mother was also distantly related by marriage to the Montreal poet Leo Kennedy (a contributor to the landmark *New Provinces* modernist anthology of 1936).

The second strand tying me to contemporary verse was a series of enrichment classes for Vancouver, B.C., high school students (one of which I had become) taught by Earle Birney at the University of B.C. on Saturday mornings in the winter of 1962. The poet energetically and carefully outlined both the mechanics and scope of contemporary poetry, infectiously conveying his enthusiasm and affection for the art form. Less than two years later the third strand began: I enrolled in UBC's Creative Writing Department. I was instructed during my time at UBC by, among others, Birney himself and by Livesay, and was introduced to another wizard of poetic narrative, Al Purdy (who visited both the campus and our class).

Other tidal forces were at work within the literary harbour that UBC was during the early 1960s, however. I arrived on campus just as the last of the student poets associated with *Tish* magazine were departing. I attended readings by these writers, and learned that there were poetries men and women could be passionate about besides what I had encountered to date. The *Tish* writers employed an approach to language far more oblique than any I had previously been exposed to.

For example, these authors placed particular emphasis on sound, and on cadence. Indeed, there was a specific *Tish* rhythm of enunciation of phrases or lines that many of the followers of this poetic displayed. Unexpected words or syllables were stressed in a sing-song manner; the result was similar to a chant during which the speaKER puts the emPHASis on the wrong syllABLE. This affectation could be gently mocked—I recall hearing a student reading the Vancouver phone book with the same odd lilting delivery invariably heard at a *Tish*ite reading. Yet the *Tish* writers taught anyone who paid sympathetic attention to them to focus on sound and rhythms in writing. These authors, like many artists determined to fully explore component aspects of their art, felt they had to develop their ideas to an extreme in order to test the range of possibilities for poetry. The enterprise overall demonstrated directions for literature that were new in that time and place.

The *Tish* poetic was very different from the straightforward narrative impetus to which I was accustomed. Puzzling and frequently unbridgeable lacunas were offered in the poetic rendition of a situation or story. However, at UBC I also had the opportunity to hear firsthand (as well as read) many of the U.S. poets who had inspired some of the compositional choices adopted by these local practitioners of the art. In the summer of 1963 I attended the evening sessions of a poetry conference on campus that brought together Charles Olson, Robert Duncan, Robert Creeley, and more. As with the *Tish* poets, I found many of the visitors' writings abstract and difficult to follow. Listening to the U.S. authors introduce their poems, though, I better understood that these writers were presenting an extract out of narrative. Story is not absent, but the audience receives only portions, moments, facets of the tale the poet tells. I was used to regarding words as a means to order my world, to enhance my enjoyment of it, to provide guidance in and understanding of my life, and to reduce my anxieties about temporal existence. These authors apparently felt confident or impish enough to play against such assumptions about words' duties to their makers and users. Their poems bounced off the solid wall of approved grammar, clear narrative, and other ordinary linguistic expectations. The poem thus might seem chaotic in diction, structure, content. But I realized thanks to the visiting poets' introductions and commentaries on their poems that this impression depends on—is in fact bonded to—the presence beyond the paper's edge or the speaker's voice of a structured, readily-apprehensible story. And by story I include the tale that customary grammar relates.

If abstract expressionist painting may be said to be "about" the stuff of painting itself—colour, shape, texture, etc.—then this literature at its least communicative could be said to be "about" the stuff of writing itself. Except that the medium from which this latter art is created, words, is inextricably melded to a rigid order of meaning, to structures that provide understanding. Words are not swirls of colour, or evocative shapes, any more than they are tones of sound. Or, more accurately, a word possesses the latter characteristic *as well as* being primarily an individual unit isolated from an invented pattern of human reason. Colours and shapes and sounds exist independently of human beings in nature; words do not.

To employ words even in the most abstract of settings is to link that setting to the purpose of words—to why humans invented and invent words, and use words each day. The Chilean poet Pablo Neruda, a master of both realism and the surreal, expressed this intent or goal for language in his 1971 Nobel Prize acceptance lecture (*Toward the Splendid City* [New York: Farrar, Straus, Giroux, 1974]) as: "to convey to others what we are"—that is, to relate a story. No escape from this defining attribute of language is achievable. Those who seek to eliminate narrative cannot do so using words.

Yet art that pushes against the received, the usual, the easy is necessary for any art form to retain vitality. However, the natural antipathy and antagonism toward the unfamiliar in art (as toward the unfamiliar in many other areas of life) is frequently enhanced, in my experience, by the exaggerated claims or other defensive postures of boundary-pushing artists. This occurrence is a shame because the focus of response shifts on both sides of the artistic argument away from the central issues of the debates necessary to prevent the stultifying of an art. I believe one source of difficulty exacerbating this unproductive scenario is the very metaphor often chosen by those artists operating on an art form's fringe: "avant-garde." This term implies that the practitioners of this approach to their arts are at the forefront of a host of writers or painters or sculptors who subsequently will trudge obediently along a path already marked and cleared. The concept reduces all artists other than the designated advance group to mere followers. As might be expected, the other artistic practitioners reject furiously this nomenclature applied to themselves.

In reality there is no identifiable host. All artists including those who deem themselves the "avant-garde" pursue their own areas of concern, whether or not influenced to some degree by any contemporary or historic set of ideas about their art. I have never met a writer who would accept the definition of herself or himself as a mainstream practitioner, passively adhering to dictums about art laid down by others. Each artist I have encountered considers herself or himself to be blazing new ground in some way.

A more helpful metaphor for the practice of art than an army on the march is to regard contemporary art as occurring on the edge of a vast, ever-expanding lumpy sphere. This globe is the assemblage of human art through the eons; every artist now alive has a place on the outer skin of the bulgy, irregular, massive amoeba. Here and there on the surface a protuberance occasionally appears involving clumps of artists — a movement. But within years or decades the sphere will have swollen so as to absorb this hump; elsewhere on the ever-growing globe new projections — minute or pronounced — have formed. The work of every living artist contributes to the expansion of the sphere. Okay, maybe there are a few places where the skin of the sphere momentarily sags inward. But this dimple or concavity, like every convexity, will vanish in the inexorable outward growth of the whole body of art. No one artist or group of artists represents a vanguard, is capable of wrenching this anarchic globe to swell only in their preferred direction. Everywhere around the circumference the sphere expands—unevenly to be sure, but unceasingly.

In a 1966 interview with Neruda (published in *Neruda and Vallejo: Selected Poems* [Boston: Beacon, 1971]), the U.S. writer Robert Bly asks the Chilean: "Why has the greatest poetry in the Twentieth Century appeared in the Spanish language?" Neruda replies: "I must tell you it is very nice to hear such a thing from an American poet. Of course we believe in enthusiasm too, but still we are all modest workers—we must not make too many comparisons." Neruda expresses in poetry as well this plea for solidarity among artists (and other human beings), in contrast to any self-anointings as the chosen one or ones. Neruda's 1968 collection *The Hands of Day* contains "This is Simple" (in Ben Belitt's translation, from *Late and Posthumous Poems 1968-1974* [New York: Grove, 1988]):

> Power is mute (the trees tell me)
> and so is profundity (say the roots)
> and purity too (says the grain).
>
> No tree ever said:
> *"I'm the tallest!"*
>
> No root ever said:
> *"I come from deeper down!"*
>
> And bread never said:
> *"What is better than bread!"*

My goal is to encourage such tolerance among my writing students each semester. I believe an attitude of open-mindedness, despite the claims made by advocates or opponents of every movement in poetry, is required in order for the students to disinterestedly ascertain which techniques can aid them in their own artistic development. In class, despite my own firm views concerning poetry's best agenda, I adopt the metaphor of "many musics," an expression I first heard from the Vancouver poet and filmmaker Colin Browne. That is, musicians and fans of music accept readily that a vast range of approaches to music—classical, jazz, blues, rock and roll, reggae, New Age and all the fusions and combinations thereof—are acceptable and enjoyable on their own terms. And so, musicians continually learn much from each other. Each practitioner is free, of course, to find this or that style of music of little personal interest. But I seldom hear a musician or fan denounce an example of their art as not being music. Instead, they merely shrug and offer something like: "Baroque is not to my taste."

One humorous bumper sticker I have observed does proclaim: "There are only two kinds of music—country and western." But *because* this slogan is considered funny, it serves as a demonstration of the tolerance that actually exists.

I confess the forbearance I preach was sorely tested between 1984 and 1987 when I was part of the core group who established the Vancouver branch of the Kootenay School of Writing. We were remnants—former staff and students—of David Thompson University Centre in Nelson, B.C., a postsecondary institution shut down by the provincial government following the sellout of the 1983 B.C. public sector general strike. Locking the doors of DTUC ended the very vibrant writing program there. In Vancouver, the majority of my fellow KSW instructors were adherents of language-centred writing. This writing views ordinary narrative as a form of closure, since obvious story in many cases can properly be read only one way. The compositional goals of language-centred writing are to create instead a sense of open-endedness, expansion, plus a distance from the confines of the "This-happened-to-*me*" tale, whether supposedly true or fictional. My KSW colleague Calvin Wharton observes, in the introduction to his and my jointly-edited *East of Main: An Anthology of Poems from East Vancouver* (Vancouver: Pulp Press, 1989), that

> [t]his poetry focusses on the *materiality* of language. ... As American poet Charles Bernstein explains, language-centered writing is "writing that takes as its medium, or domain of intention, every articulable aspect of language." ... Language-centered writing ... [claims] that writing is always a construction, is never *real*, and consequently this must be acknowledged. ...
>
> In these works, "the sum of the text is not reducible to any one of its statements," as U.S. poet Ron Silliman says. A poem ... does not peak on a single line or statement, the way many narrative poems build to a crescendo ending. This writing ..., as Bernstein emphasizes, has "... a tendency that can pull a poem out of the realm of purely personal reference and into a consideration of the interaction among the seemingly competing spheres of politics, autobiography, fiction, philosophy, common sense, song, etc."

The products of this type of writing attain for me an impenetrable denseness. At best, reading or listening to them is like strolling along a busy street catching fragments of dozens of simultaneous, unrelated conversations. An example of this poetry at its worst occurred at one session of a conference, the New Poetics Colloquium, we at KSW hosted in August of 1985 that brought Canadians interested in language-centred writing together with U.S. luminaries of the Language poetry movement like Bernstein, Silliman, Susan Howe, and Lyn Hejinian. One poet began his allotted reading by setting a small alarm clock on the lectern. He opened a folder containing a manuscript and began to intone his material. After ten minutes or so, with the audience lulled into a semi-soporific state, we were abruptly jerked into consciousness by the shrill insistent clamour of the alarm. The reader coolly shut off the noise, and closed his folder. "That's enough of that," he announced. He opened a second manuscript folder, and began to read something else. Since beginnings and endings play no significant part in his compositional principles, where he started or finished his reading of a text was of no consequence. What was important was the duration of our exposure to his writing, not any specific passage or passages.

Of course, practitioners of any movement in writing—even ones I feel strongly attached to—can behave at the microphone in a goofy and counterproductive manner. I was more interested in learning what audiences receive from listening to an hour or more of the non-sequential sentences and free-floating phrases that comprise a reading of language-centred texts. I was cheered to observe that most audience response registered around the puns that appear from time to time in the flow of dissociated language—puns being the closest approach to humour that this kind of writing usually permits itself. A pun here is an island of linguistic narrative in a sea of fractured or disconnected talk. After all, a pun makes two clear statements—tells two stories—and the comedy arises from the shock of the gap between the two. I was heartened by the evident relief of the audience in reaching the solid ground of story. And, unsurprisingly, conventional prose narrative is required for the proponents of Language poetry to explain their beliefs. Those who seek to discredit narrative cannot do so by means of words.

Elsewhere I've written about a central question for me with regard to this and other poetry that is determinately difficult of access: what are the *uses* of obscurity, political as well as artistic? That is, what effect is created in the reader/listener? Can this effect be verified? Why is this effect a goal desired by the writer? In an era when communication with words is everywhere debased to human detriment—by governments, corporations, and mass entertainment—why should poets abandon the struggle to clearly and accurately articulate our lives? At a historical moment when serious poetry is marginalized, how is the health of the art form aided by a poetic that only a highly specialized handful of people can comprehend?

Luckily, these are questions I have to answer only for myself; debates around narrative or other aspects of poetic composition are ones I do not have to win, except internally. One of my KSW colleagues, Jeff Derksen, has pursued language-centred writing and won the 1991 B.C. poetry prize in doing so. I remember once in a discussion with him being startled by his comment: "We are all realists, Tom." His style of writing, on which my mind can get no purchase, is nevertheless his attempt to reproduce reality as he believes the literary arts can best convey it. In that goal we are united.

The Oregon poet (and former Consultant in Poetry to the Library of Congress) William Stafford describes in an interview in *The American Poetry Review* (25.3 [May/June 1993]) how he dislikes "experimental" poetry when it leads a writer into a programmatic frame of mind, away from her or his true self. The interviewer asks for a response from Stafford about the Language poets. Stafford replies:

> I think this might seem a little strange coming from me because I am a language-that-I-meet-when-I-talk-to-the-mailman kind of poet, but experiments in the language, the Language poets seem as interesting as any other experiments, but no more. And I already said what I think about experimenters. To have a program is to abandon art. Right and left, I'm not there, you know, I'm here in the center.

He continues to emphasize that a writer must hold fast to individual truths, including the choice of whatever forms are judged by that author as most suitable to depict those truths. The interviewer is pressuring Stafford to reveal his "plan" for writing. To Stafford, the process of composition is more organic, more grounded in who he is. He states:

> A person is lost in the woods; they bring a tracker to find this person. The tracker brings his bloodhound in the back of his pick-up. The journalist or critic comes up to the bloodhound and says: "Mr. bloodhound, what is your plan?" The bloodhound goes *Sniff sniff sniff sniff*. The critic says, "I mean, you know, you must have a principle on this to find this person." The bloodhound's going *Sniff sniff sniff sniff*. I'm the bloodhound. The critic wants to have a plan.

The Ontario poet Bronwen Wallace provides a spirited defense of staying faithful to a poetic born out of her own considered history, experiences, preferences. In a 1986 epistolary debate with the Montreal writer Erin Mouré (excerpted in *Quarry* [42:2; 1993] and more fully published in *Two Women Talking* [Toronto: League of Canadian Poets, 1993]), Wallace defends her choice of narrative style against attacks by feminist and language-based critics suggested to her by Mouré.

> Examining language is important, obviously, and provides the basis for an important feminist *methodology. ... It is not a dogma.* There is no one way to go about it, no one goal. It is not the *only* subversive or revolutionary act. We're all of us in the wild zone; there's more than one way through. ... Let's not kid ourselves. Language-centred writing can be just as easily co-opted by the patriarchy as any other kind.

In a subsequent letter, Wallace attests to her ardent embrace of coherent, accessible story:

> The given, of *my* life, the starting point of my *poetry* has always been the stories of women, the voices of women discussing the world. From as early as I can remember it was my grandmother, my mother, my aunts, my girl friends, my women friends, female teachers and mentors who spoke the world for me. My grandmother and my mother were ... both subject and object, powerful and powerless. And when they talked! They used gossip, confession, anecdote, jokes—but they used them to tell their experience of the world, to create a world in which the female was the metaphor for the universal. ...
> Much, much of my own work—in fact the essence of my narrative style—has come from these women's lives and the stories they told. What I try to do is to recreate their voices, their view of things, their way of telling a story. When I do

this I am "facing the question of language." I am looking at the language politically. An analogy might be the work of Heather Bishop or Ferron, neither of whom challenge the limits of folk-rock very radically, but both of whom use musical language politically. ...

So when Barbara Godard [author of an article in the Jan. 1984 issue of *Room of One's Own* that Mouré has sent Wallace] says that native women and black women are "not ready to face the question of language, but this hasn't been true in Quebec ...," she is being patronizing and dogmatic. She is implying that they (or lower class, rural women like my grandmother and mother, myself—my roots) are not facing language *her way*. But we're still facing it.

And when [Kathy] Mezei [another contributor to the Jan. 1984 issue of *Room of One's Own*] talks about going "beyond talking about realism" there's a sense throughout the article that realism is somehow pejorative. Who says? Why?

To Neruda, as to Stafford, the point is to resolve these matters for oneself, not to become embroiled in an attempt to convince others to adopt one's own conclusions. He declares in his Nobel lecture:

When all is said, there is no individual poet who administers poetry, and if a poet sets himself up to accuse his fellows, or if some other poet wastes his life in defending himself against reasonable or unreasonable charges, it is my conviction that only vanity can so mislead us. I consider the enemies of poetry are to be found not among those who practice poetry or guard it, but in mere lack of agreement in the poet.

Neruda, however, in his very next sentence apparently contradicts himself. He continues: "For this reason, no poet has any considerable enemy other than his own incapacity to make himself understood by the most forgotten and exploited of his contemporaries, and this applies to all epochs and in all countries." Even though I entirely agree with Neruda's sentiment in favour of clear speaking and choice of ideal audience, he implies that a poet who adopts an opaque use of language is necessarily in a dispute with herself or himself. I cannot agree with *this* conclusion.

Yet because Neruda observes that each poet will articulate, rightly or wrongly, her or his own artistic vision, I will conclude by sketching mine. My goal is to develop *narratives* that more accurately than ever before depict our human relationships and interrelationships. These stories must of necessity begin with daily work, the means for human survival and the point at which we contribute to the continuation of our community, including the reproduction of its power relationships (for good or ill). Enmeshed with work, though, are all the tangled webs and networks of family, nature, and the myriad of social constructs we classify as politics, leisure, entertainment, spiritual beliefs. Each aspect here interconnects with every other. "The personal is political," the women's movement has proclaimed. But that equation is only one string in a skein. For example, the political is no less economic, as Marx showed so long ago. And the economic is bound up with technology, geography, history, ecology and much more (including the personal).

The amazing intricacies of human relationships and interactions spiralling outward from the work we do will provide endless subject matter for poets. These connections and arrangements and rearrangements suggest to me an enormous cycle of narratives yet untold, incipient poetries.

Whatever my vision, though, poets will write in whatever manner they choose, even if I disagree as vehemently with their creative choices as they with mine. Our shared challenge is the limits of our common artistic medium—words and a grammar that makes possible the sharing of meaning, But an art that does not reveal how daily work in any age shapes both personal and community life fails to accurately express either the individual or communal story. This is similar to how an art that ignores the roles and social status of women in any age fails to accurately express either the individual or communal story. Meanwhile the labour of *both* women and men reproduces the world each day, and that employment contains the potential opportunity to build a better community than the day before.

Of course there are other uses for art than to tell the human story: escape, play, exploration of the art's media, depicting the world in a startlingly fresh way, and so on. But an art form in any age when considered as a whole also tells a story, constitutes a narrative. The values such a narrative expresses are vital to a people's understanding of themselves. Where daily work is judged to have little or no consequence, no significant part in that tale, the story is incomplete, misleading, and a contributor to our daily servitude.

I CAN FEEL
_____ **THE FUTURE TREMBLING** _____
Official Dreams, Dreams of Work

My experiences in the 1960s convinced me the dreams of individuals shape society. The educational policies we young people opposed were once simply the visions of men and women who saw schools as a place to inculcate the factory virtues: obedience to arbitrary authority, acceptance of boredom, adjustment to daily life in a prison of measured time. The economic arrangements we opposed are the realization of the dreams of owners and managers: to be free to use the biosphere—people, plants, animals, air, soil, water—to maximize financial gains for themselves and the enterprises and institutions they control. Governments, in this vision, are a source of public wealth to tap into as needed—for tax forgiveness, or outright cash subsidies. Governments also serve as a publicly funded enabler in the service of private gain—to help break strikes, say, or to wage war on recalcitrant foreign competitors or reluctant foreign consumers.

We young people in the 1960s did not overturn our society's power relations, but we did disturb them. And I observed how fast an individual's values can change when her or his vision alters. In months, young men and women I knew went from support for the Vietnam War to an activist stance against it, often accompanied by a growing awareness of that overseas conflict not as an aberration but as a *consequence* of their society's prevailing attitudes toward human beings. Change was in the air: when I began graduate school in Southern California's Orange County in 1966 you could get your car tires slashed for displaying the peace sign on your bumper; when I graduated in 1968 you could purchase in department stores earrings and clothing that featured the same symbol. As self-confidence grips an energetic segment of the population as in the 1960s, officially approved dreams can be discarded rapidly. Eastern Europe in the 1990s is not the only place and time where a society's apparently entrenched values disappeared in what seemed an instant.

I draw two conclusions from witnessing such a hasty abandonment of previously held concepts and mores. First, most of us sleep-walk through our roles in the official version of reality, even if we accede to them. This behaviour may account for why people under the right circumstances can replace many of their beliefs with stunning speed. Second, abruptly acquiring a critical perspective on official dreams results in emotional shock. A rock lyric of the 1960s (David Clayton-Thomas' "Brainwashed") reflects my conclusions:

> I woke up one morning and I took a look around:
> Found myself living in the city dog pound.
> Told myself this just can't be
> In the home of the brave and the land of the free.

I experienced for the second time a sudden social transformation of my fellow citizens in the autumn of 1983, during B.C.'s public sector general strike. This event was a reaction to a provincial austerity budget involving reductions in public service employment and government programs of every sort, as well as the freezing of wages for government employees. The B.C. strike was an escalating one, bringing out in a predetermined sequence a different group of public sector workers every few days, starting with teachers. Incrementally, more and more of the functions of government ceased to exist.

As the walkout swelled, the employees on strike felt their power. My component, the faculty association of a community college in a Vancouver suburb, met continually to discuss the strike and to vote to reaffirm our participation. From statements made in these gatherings, and in public strike support meetings I attended in Vancouver, I could watch people's attitudes quickly change. The success of our common venture freed dreams that had been suppressed for years, or that had never before assumed concrete form. This alteration arose in part from the validation of our cause provided by the tangible popular support shown us while we were on picket duty. Neighbours spontaneously brought coffee and food to picketers at local schools, and neighbours opened their homes to us for respite from the continual chill autumn rain that drenched us every shift on the line. In house windows throughout the city I saw pro-strike banners, signs, and placards displayed. In downtown Vancouver, strangers who were wearing compatible buttons would stop each other on the street to exchange the latest news. Given how the media covered the strike, alternative sources of information sprang up: friends telephoned friends elsewhere in the province to learn firsthand what actually was happening in Prince Rupert, in Kamloops, in the Kootenays. These discoveries were shared at strike meetings, or face-to-face on the soggy lines. Women and men involved with the strike also expressed mutual reassurance that together we were helping create a non-violent, moral response to official bullying, to a vision of society that justifies the weak being preyed upon by the strong.

While the strike held and expanded, every social subject was introduced for discussion at the incessant support meetings. For the first time ever, I heard people question in public: "Where do we go when we move past resisting what has been imposed on us?" "What do we need a government for?" "What do we need the legislature for?" "What do we need political parties for?" And even—or especially—"What are unions good for?" Alternative methods of organizing a self-governing society, different from a Westminster-style parliamentary system and

AFL-CIO business unionism, started to be proposed and explored, albeit in a desultory way.

These were heady hours. As the numbers of women and men on strike and engaged in strike support increased, Ralph Chaplin's words were felt in the bones of hundreds of thousands of B.C. citizens: "Without our brain and muscle not a single wheel can turn" ("Solidarity Forever").

Yet the shock that the alterations in belief which involvement in the strike churned up also found expression. B.C. author Leona Gom, at the time a community college faculty colleague of mine, opens her poem "November" with: "it has always happened somewhere else." She ends:

> we have lived here too long
> to pretend we are still
> tourists taking
> notes for a book,
> with somewhere safe to go home to.
> this time it is ourselves
> on the picket lines,
> we are cold and frightened and
> tired, and changed in a way
> we will never forgive.

Compared to the 1960s, this moment of possibility was brief. The strike was betrayed at the height of its success by the B.C. Federation of Labour leadership. Signs, placards, buttons, ideas disappeared from public view within twenty-four hours as though confiscated. A few days after the sellout, people resumed talking about sports, soap operas, television sit-coms.

As in the late 1960s, however, during the general strike time itself was transformed. A new agenda for daily life was taking shape, however rudimentarily; other dreams of how society could function were clumsily and haltingly rising through the mists of social sleep. Each day vibrated with fresh choices; victories and setbacks in our collective effort toward a better life were experienced, talked over, evaluated, reformulated. Boundaries in people's thinking were crossed, and the impact of our actions in collectively altering the normal functioning of society was both exhilarating and scary. Each activity of daily life — from the most basic individual task like cooking breakfast, to more complicated social chores like comparing teaching techniques with colleagues while walking our picket shift in the drenching rain — glowed and pulsed with alternatives. The given, the customary, was no longer sacrosanct; ideas and procedures that I would find more enjoyable than what I was used to floated just ahead of me, us. Dino Valenti of the rock band Quicksilver Messenger Service had expressed something of this sensation of the imminence of, as well as the threat to, significant social change a decade and a half previously in "What About Me":

> I work in your factories, and I study in your schools;
> I fill your penitentiaries and your military, too.
> I can feel the future trembling as the word is passed round.
> If you stick up for what you do believe in, be prepared to
> be shot down.

Slogans from the Paris May Days of 1968 seemed revitalized as goals: "Live without dead time;" "Under the pavement, the beach."

With the sellout of the 1983 strike, all the malevolence of the approved vision of the 1980s, 1990s and afterward descended. Engineered increases in poverty, in social meanness, in corporate profits, in the gap between the comfortable and the poor. An engineered reduction in the quality of individual and common life.

As I write this, I have been alive more than half a century. Now when I dream of a better society, I imagine three interconnected processes combining to enhance my everyday existence.

The first process is an ongoing debate concerning the *purpose* of the community or society in which I live. As I maintain in my collection of essays, *A Country Not Considered: Canada, Culture, Work* (Toronto: Anansi, 1993), we need to openly describe what we think

Canada (or our local neighbourhood) is *for*. In the passage I quote below, I am responding to the reduction of government support for Canadian culture. To me, trying to examine this national issue—and many others—without a clear statement from each speaker about what he or she sees as the reason for *having* a nation—not to mention this *particular* nation—is like critiquing an example of architecture without considering the building's purpose.

> In other words, what is Canada *for*? Does it primarily exist to provide a place where men and women who own enterprises can maximize profits? Or is it intended to be a sort of cooperative venture, whereby all those who live here work jointly to ensure the maximum happiness for one another? ...
>
> Or is the nation's aim to provide a free and democratic environment in which the people who live here can make their own decisions and solve their own problems? If so, how far should this democracy extend?

I have altered my opinion often enough on sundry matters throughout the years to realize that disagreement, conflicting views, is an indication of health in any organization or movement for social change. Argument allows me to test out the limits and soundness of my beliefs, my dreams. I will present my case as strongly as possible, and try as hard as I can to win you over to my viewpoint. Still, *debate* on the purpose of the society we are constructing is my aim—not unanimity, not one solution, not one correct answer.

The second process I wish implemented, however, is for me a non-negotiable prerequisite for human happiness: the democratization of work. What happens to us on the job is not peripheral, but pivotal, to our community. A society only functions as the result of each of us going through the activities every day that collectively we call "work." It is in the simplest acts we perform each day on the job that we reproduce all the social relationships that exist in our community—from the creation and distribution of wealth to the institutionalization of sexism and racism.

Yet one of capitalism's rousing successes has been to diminish people's sense of themselves as producers, and vastly inflate our sense of ourselves as consumers. Even where social activists have, over time, created structural inroads into capitalist society such as the legalization of unions or the construction of a social safety net, the ingenuity and efficacy of capitalism has managed to convince us to regard these accomplishments with the eye of a consumer and not a producer—to ask ourselves: what can I get out of these organizations or opportunities and how little do I have to contribute in order to gain the maximum benefit?

Meanwhile, the undemocratic nature of how employment is presently organized results in a personal experience of daily life that can only be categorized as bizarre. In the introduction to my 1993 selected poems, I describe how part of each day we inhabit a social space in which democratic principles supposedly apply. Then—on passing through the time tunnel of the office door or factory gate—we become residents of an era when persons of our social status have not yet attained the right to vote. "We are expected to alternate every few hours between being freedom-loving, responsible citizens of a democratic community while off the job, and docile, unquestioning respecters of authority while at work," the introduction points out. This constant shuttling between two fundamentally different sets of values, two diametrically opposed senses of ourselves, has to be crazy-making.

Since work is where society is reproduced each day, how wholesome a community can be built by people desperately struggling to resolve within themselves two contradictory visions? And the absence of an accurate depiction of daily employment in our educational, artistic, commercial or political discourses exacerbates an already unhealthy situation. Behavioural theory teaches that denial of a family dysfunction like child abuse or alcoholism compounds the problems such conduct causes. In the same manner, the blanket of silence that virtually every facet of our society has thrown around our state of unfreedom at work only makes worse the damaging behaviours we adopt to cope with the situation our employment imposes on us.

Thus, the third and final process I am convinced is necessary for a better society is the monitoring by ourselves of our patterns of behaviour. As I have previously written about, one of the difficulties in implementing workplace freedom is people like me. Social change has to be made with damaged goods: men and women negatively affected by their responses to the lack of freedom they endure at the heart of the day.

Public education about the causes and effects of the behavioural patterns of each of us, and of the institutions we are involved with, is vital to an improved society. A comparatively recent body of knowledge about interpersonal behaviours has much to inform us about achieving happier lives at both the personal and public levels. How an enterprise or organization I am part of functions, how I respond to attending a meeting or to a personal confrontation, what I expect a spouse or family to offer me, how comfortable I am with intimacy are all influenced by my own behaviours. These behaviours may well have external sources, but my happiness in social no less than private life depends on my understanding of the ways my activities and words contribute to providing me with an environment I enjoy or am numbed by or hate.

These, then, are the three processes—three clusters of attitudes, objectives and acts—that together comprise my vision of a society in which I believe I would feel more fulfilled, more at home. All three endeavours influence my engagement in social issues and organizations. But another factor—more to do with tactics than strategy—modifies my involvement in public life This factor is my assessment of my past participation in various social struggles: my weighing of what I have found helpful and not helpful in creating societal change either in the microcosm or macrocosm.

I no longer believe in the traditional Five P's of social activism: posters, pickets, petitions, pamphlets, parades. These five dreary and ultimately ineffective approaches are hauled out and recycled as the remedy for virtually every issue. The authorities, no less than ourselves, know their assigned part in the dance of the Five P's. The whole scenario often becomes a "your turn to curtsy, my turn to bow" ritual: eventual confrontations, some arrests (occasionally even accompanied by legitimate charges of brutality), some court time, maybe fines (or even an occasional minor jail sentence), and everybody on both sides can go home feeling perfectly satisfied. Meanwhile, the machine grinds on.

I now believe effective opposition is a matter of questioning: "Where are they vulnerable? Where can they be hurt the most?" Usually this is a matter of heeding the advice of Watergate's Deep Throat: "Follow the money." Any government can absorb without flinching any number of one-shot street protests, no matter how these might snarl traffic or inconvenience consumers for a single day. What strategies and tactics might have more impact? Instituting and maintaining a consumer boycott of the products or services offered by companies owned by government members or by the government's significant financial supporters? Without question, as the B.C. public sector general strike showed, when there is no public service there is no government. The legislature merely becomes a few expensive suits and dresses talking to one another in an old stone building.

A protest on the legislature lawn cedes to the government our power, which lies always with ourselves—individually, in how we live, and collectively, in where we are employed. To be forever in opposition is to always be engaged by others' dreams. No one who takes our power will be swayed by sweet reason, and spontaneously give us a better life. Just as today our actions on the job and in the community and in the family fashion the structures we wish to change, so our actions each day on the job and in the community and in the family are the only place we can build the new world we desire. Why do we put so much effort year after year into realizing the dreams of other people—people who obviously do not have our best interests in mind? Our attempts to improve the future, though, must fall far short of our goal unless we fundamentally alter the core of our common existence, the main source of the dreams that entangle us, that drag us down. We need to get to work.

I'LL SAY THIS
Interviews

AFFIRMATIVE POETRY

An Interview with Andrew McEwan
for *Acta Victoriana* (2010)

When did you first know you wanted to be a poet?

I don't know that I ever "wanted to be a poet." My career goal when I entered UBC was to be an astrophysicist. But university math (for example, calculating the surface area of a three-dimensional object like a donut) proved daunting. I then intended to be a journalist. I found I enjoyed working on the student newspaper, *The Ubyssey*, which at the time was the farm team for the main downtown newspaper, *The Vancouver Sun* (no relation to the Toronto *Sun,* but more like the *Toronto Star*). Many of us on *The Ubyssey* worked four months each summer on *The Sun,* and some *Ubyssey* staffers worked a shift each week during the academic year.

I took creative writing courses at UBC because I thought the experience would enhance my writing skills as a reporter. However, when I graduated from UBC I won a Woodrow Wilson Fellowship, so decided to go to grad school in creative writing at the University of California at Irvine. I saw this as a brief break before descending into a lifetime career as a reporter. Instead, the experience totally changed me, in part because my stint in graduate school occurred in southern California during the 1960s.

I first became interested in *writing* poetry in high school, like so many other people (as a means to sort through adolescent angst). I somehow read Lawrence Lipton's *The Holy Barbarians* (1959), about beatniks living in Venice, a Los Angeles suburb, and that book included examples of beat poetry. I already knew there were alternatives to the kind of rhymed-and-metred poetry I'd been exposed to in school: my parents, who grew up in Toronto, were personally acquainted with the various left-wing poets such as Earle Birney, Dorothy Livesay and Miriam Waddington, and our house when I was growing up in Prince Rupert, B.C. and Vancouver always had the latest Canadian poets' volumes, including works by Eli Mandel, Irving Layton, Leonard Cohen, Margaret Avison, and so on. But the beats were more free-form in style and content than even the free-verse poetry I had read, and such freedom was appealing to me as a teenager.

By the time I had been through UBC's and UC Irvine's creative writing workshops, and had begun to publish, I was more ready to consider myself seriously engaged in poetry. But by then I knew the term "poet," like the designation "artist," is used by a variety of people for a variety of purposes—not all benign. I balked at considering myself "a poet" for a very long period. I like to write and publish, and I call some of what I write "poems." Yet some part of me regards wanting to be a "poet" like wanting to be a real estate "developer" or a "manager of a hedge fund"—an admission of soul-sickness. What I want is to write good poems.

In the introduction to Did I Miss Anything?: Selected Poems 1973-1993 *you cite Eliot as a primary international influence on you. You describe how your poem "Asphalt Hours, Asphalt Air" is an attempt to "banish [Eliot's] dry darkness forever" from your poetry. To do this you rewrote* The Waste Land, *incorporating "North American industrial and societal myths." What role do you feel you have, as a poet, to build on tradition or to "banish" it?*

To put my remark in context: I was an Honours English student at UBC in an era when T.S. Eliot held the position in criticism that the

French and other postmodern critics hold today. At the University of Calgary where I taught for some years, it's rare to receive an application to grad school, or to vet a SSHRC application, that doesn't somehow work in a reference to or quotation from Derrida or Foucault or Bakhtin, etc. As Honours English students we were the same, except our point of reference was Eliot. What's dreary about this automatic invocation of critical authority is the utter predictability of the reference, and the attitude of abjection that students (including me in my former life) must take toward critics held up as models. Even when we disagreed with some point or other, the critic's supposed place in the pantheon was unquestionable. Today, Eliot is utterly forgotten as a critical influence, just as in a generation English students will cackle with glee at the absurdities of postmodernist shibboleths—if a student happens to come upon a footnote that refers to any such critical concepts.

However, and this is an important distinction with regard to the postmodernists, Eliot walked the walk as well as talked the talk. He not only would tell you what constituted important literature, he produced it. How many poems by Derrida or Irigaray (in translation, to be sure) are in your anthologies? *The Waste Land* and the adventures of Mr. Prufrock were held up to us as shining examples of what literature should do.

Eliot and his chum Pound were decidedly right-wing writers (anti-Semitic, reactionary; Pound was a dedicated Fascist). And postmodernism was introduced into the universities at the exact moment when students at such institutions were threatening the social order. Students in the 1960s were a societal force not because of what they thought, said and wrote, but because they *acted* on their beliefs on campus and off, and because they clearly were organizing themselves to further transform society.

Of course, postmodernism incorporates some anti-establishment lip service, just as Fascism in its various forms included a leftist veneer. Unions were part of the Italian corporate state, Hitler's organization was called the National Socialist German Workers' Party, and the Nazi SA (*Sturmabteilung*) Brownshirts (later violently suppressed by Hitler) were popularly known as "beefsteaks"—brown on the outside, red in the middle. Similarly postmodernism can sport a veneer of social critique. Yet as a means of social control, postmodernism has been far more successful than Eliot's ideas proved to be: universities have been transformed from sites from which social critique spilled into action in the wider society, as students participated (and spearheaded, in some instances) the civil rights, anti-Vietnam war, anti-imperialist and women's movements. Today's students, while mouthing platitudes about the evils of capitalism, quietly seek institutional certification that will ensure them academic or commercial or artistic careers (usually supported directly or indirectly by tax dollars gathered and dispensed by the capitalist state).

For all Eliot's wonderfully artistic literary collages, the message of social defeat and despair and class hatred is evident to any reader. Traditionally in English, poetry mainly has been produced by those with the education and leisure (indicating an elevated position in a social hierarchy) to produce it. The subjects chosen by practitioners of the literary arts, and the subjects omitted in our literature, reflect who gets to produce art and who gets to praise art, as the women's movement has shown. Eliot was in the long line of that literary tradition, both in his critical and creative modes. The role I see for myself, and tried to wrestle with in "Asphalt Hours," is to understand the strengths and weaknesses of that tradition, and to move art to engage different, more socially beneficial goals.

In "Asphalt Hours, Asphalt Air" you, like Eliot, make extensive use of quotations, but yours seem to come from various working speakers. In what sense do you feel poetry—specifically work poetry—has an obligation to speak for other people in one's community, city, country, etc.?
Despite all the good advice I freely dispense, I know that artists (including poets) will follow what interests them about their art form. So I'd never say that poetry "has an obligation" to do anything. Because of the accidental timing of my birth, however, I witnessed the important role that poetry played in the civil rights movement, the anti-Vietnam War movement, the women's movement. Also, during the brief period in

the late 1960s and early 1970s when the Canadian ruling class decided it was in their economic interests to have a country of their own, and so launched the explosion of state funding for Canadian culture, such as the Canada Council's aid to publishers, etc., a new book of poems by Layton or Al Purdy was a real media event. The attention paid to these new books was not based on how much money the author would receive, like the hoopla currently generated over the Giller or the Griffin Prizes. Instead, attention was focused on what the poems *said* and how they said it—on form, and especially content.

So my experience has been that clear speaking is a means to engage a wider community than literary specialists. I don't think plain-spoken poetry was *crucial* to the social movements I mention. Yet poetry was regarded within these movements as an essential form of expression of the participants' dreams and fears, successes and setbacks, strengths and flaws.

I believe one of the goals for the introduction of postmodernism into the humanities was to make sure that students—including the artists of tomorrow—cannot speak the same language as the larger community, and thus to sever the link between campus and community. Originally, the academy spoke Latin while the laity spoke the vernacular, the exact parallel to how today's bright young minds all too often speak jargon while the community around them uses language differently. The burgeoning activist link in the late 1960s between campus and community led to such status-quo-shaking events as the Paris May Days of 1968 (the alliance between intellectuals, including students, and the labour movement), and the explosion of revulsion against the U.S. invasion of Cambodia in May 1970 that saw hundreds of U.S. campuses having to be shut by police and troops (and led to the fatal shooting of student protesters at Kent State and Jackson State). By contrast, despite the postmodern critiques of capitalist society docilely memorized by students today, Canada's military intervention into the Afghan civil war on behalf of a corrupt and vicious narco-administration battling a tribal movement led by religious psychopaths, with both sides heavily involved in the heroin trade, occurred without much of a peep from the universities.

I'd stress that, for *me*, poetry needs to not only listen to the wider community beyond the academic and literary (hence the quotations in "Asphalt Hours"), but also to speak *to* (not speak *for*) the wider community. The success of the work poems has been their articulation (including via quotations) of the central and governing experience of most people's lives—their jobs. Always, though, the work poems of merit for me speak with an *insider's* eye—either through the poet's own experiences, or careful research. That is, the poems speak from *within* (though not on behalf of) the broader community.

To understand a community is to understand how it organizes its daily reproduction—the conditions under which the distribution of goods, services, privilege, decision-making and wealth is undertaken. People in the work force know a tremendous amount—not just practical information and skills. Abstract reasoning is part of every job, as, for example, Mike Rose has eloquently shown in *The Mind at Work* (Penguin, 2004). Unlike academics, journeyed tradespeople have to constantly requalify as current in their field, including steadily taking mandatory courses and passing mandatory exams. Quotations that demonstrate this on-the-job knowledge have the potential, I believe, to broaden and deepen people's understanding of their own achievements, of their latent power. This is no different than how the poetry of the women's movement in its earlier stages incorporated both the experiences of the poet and of other women, accurately reported and clearly articulated.

But the aim of such writing as I advocate is to encourage beneficial social change. If one's personal objective for one's writing is to have a literary career, to enhance one's social and economic standing at the expense of the larger community (those tax dollars again), then what I suggest as needful for poetry will make no sense. Hence, again, my reluctance to declare any "obligation" for artists.

If so, do you see your editorial work on poetry anthologies to be an extension of this goal?
Certainly. My anthologies, as I have stated in their introductions and elsewhere, gather together poems that fit my critical standards: the

work poems that I have assembled display an insider's eye, focus on specific detail from the job (and thus demonstrate the range of knowledge that goes into the most apparently routine tasks) and frequently include humour (which is how most of us get through the working day). Other anthologists have collected poems which, to me, are *about* work but not *from* a specific workplace. These may be fine poems, but if I'm editing, they won't make the cut.

Ideally, any anthology (whether of work literature, Canadian literature, women's literature, immigrant literature, etc.) allows a reader to decide for herself or himself whether the authors as a group are moved by certain themes, artistic forms, beliefs about society or art or anything else. Of course, the editor of the anthology has a big influence on what a reader takes away from the experience of encountering the volume. Hence the battles over the literary canon: who needs to be read, in order to accurately reflect an era or a geographical location or a theme? Is the range and/or quality of *poems* the most important aspect of a poetry anthology, or is what matters the demographics of the *contributors*?

My goal with the work poems anthologies is the extension of democracy to the workplace. Liberation of the workplace is important because the job is where society is refashioned each day by the simplest acts of ourselves and our fellow-employees. We reproduce all the power arrangements by consenting to them one more day, in return for the money we need to live. We are assured by our rulers that we are free citizens of a democracy, whose opinions matter in the shaping of the community's aims and actions—except, er, where we really shape the community's aims and actions each day. No wonder the citizenry behaves so irrationally, caught in the endless daily schizophrenic shuffle between freedom and servitude.

An anthology accurately depicting not only what happens to us at work, but also how our employment affects our hours off the job, seems to me a contribution to human liberation by demonstrating—implicitly, if not overtly—the task that still lies before us of democratizing the workplace.

In your essay "An Aspirin as Big as the Sun," you mention that your work poetry came out of a tradition of political poetry. Were there writers before you that you took as examples for your new work poetics?
My first anthology, *Beaton Abbot's Got the Contract* (NeWest, 1974), contained some of these first positive models. Although I hadn't yet stepped back from the poems I had gathered, and decided how to think about them as a whole (to "theorize," in the current jargon), this first anthology includes poems by Milton Acorn, Purdy, and Pablo Neruda (in translation). As negative examples—poems to avoid—I saw how the 1930s "proletarian" art movements often omit an accurate depiction of daily work in favour of talking instead about *class*, or about moments when work *stops*, for example, strikes. These latter topics didn't interest me as much as seeing what a range of people working at every sort of job had to say about what happens to them at work and also how their employment influences their time between quitting for the day and showing up for work again.

What, in the medium of poetry, do you find particularly effective in addressing the issues of employment hierarchies and working life that is distinct from other forms of writing and art?
On every job, including teaching in postsecondary institutions, people relate pertinent stories that encapsulate the absurdities of how our society organizes daily work by means of imposed (unelected) hierarchies of *power*, rather than by means of, say, hierarchies of *knowledge* (such as those that form spontaneously in instances of free labour, for instance when a group of volunteers build a dock at a church camp). So the anecdote—which poetry among all the other arts is best suited to capture—is a particularly useful form with which to articulate the experience of employment.

Poetry's potential to effectively address any social issue also derives from poetry's potential brevity (in an era when people are bombarded with demands on their time), poetry's potential lyricism (in an era when human emotion is sanitized and sold back to us in the form of advertising), and poetry's potential articulation of the self (in an era when, despite Facebook "friends" and other mediated connections, people feel more isolated than ever—so much so that they often fear unmediated time spent alone with the selves they hardly know).

The speakers of your poems often employ the diction of everyday speech. Does the underlying goal of work poetry demand the clear articulation that such poetics enables, or could there conceivably be work poetry divorced from this style?

Despite my own artistic preferences, I agree there could "conceivably be work poetry divorced from" clear diction. I can't imagine what the advantage of speaking about work in this manner would be. But one of the delights of art is that it constantly surprises.

In many of your work poems you include the specific names of people you are speaking about, referring to them directly. What do you find is the value of employing names in poetry?

Use of other people's names reminds the reader that while the poet— whose name we are given—may be creating a world via words, the real planet has billions of people on it, people whose views and experiences likely differ from the author's. As well, when a tree is described in a poem, naming a specific species like "Douglas fir" creates a different impression on a reader than referring to a generalization like "evergreen." In the same way, use of an individual's name suggests that even though we sometimes regard the world around us as a generalized blur, the place we inhabit is in fact made up of discrete specifics. The U.S. poet Robert Bly has written about how numbing for poetry is what he terms "plural consciousness": seeing everything as general categories, rather than, as he puts it, "one leaf at a time, one Lutheran at a time, one apartment door at a time." Specific names suggest the individual, not the category, even if the poem is using the individual named to convey some generalized thought.

In regards to names in your poetry, you often refer to yourself in the third person (as "Wayman"), which seems distinct from other writers. What do you find useful about this device, compared to using the first person "I"?

Any "I" in writing—whether autobiographical or not—is a constructed, fictional character. Unfortunately, some writers know so intimately the "I" they are attempting to convey that they don't take the time to construct that character in their poem: the character comes across as flat, or a reader may conclude something quite different about the "I" than the author intends. Naming the "I" after myself helped remind me that for the character to mean anything to the reader I had to portray the dimensions of that character.

The named "I" character turned out to have a comic side to it, as well. So the "Wayman" character was often used by me in poems that started out as complaints but turned into humorous pieces in the process of composition. Eventually these poems became a shtick so I stopped writing them. The high point for this usage was when Thistledown Press liked the concept so much that they issued an entire book of "Wayman" poems, *The Nobel Prize Acceptance Speech* (1981), and even hired an illustrator for the volume. As I say, though, enough was enough and I haven't used this device for decades now.

Your work poetry seems to make its critiques by affirming the daily jobs and lives of workers within the systems of employment. What do you see as the strength of affirmative poetry, rather than critical poetry that has the same goal?

K. Linda Kivi, who edited *The Purcell Suite*, a 2007 anthology of fiction, nonfiction and poetry published in opposition to the mega-ski resort proposed for Jumbo Pass in B.C.'s Purcell Mountains, says that in order for people to want to work to save the environment, they have to love it. So not a single piece in the volume attacks the proposed resort, discussing, for instance, the hideous impact the immense project (several thousand beds) would have on the wildlife corridor in which it is to be situated. Instead, each contribution expresses some writer's interactions with the glories of the Purcells and of the Rocky Mountain trench of which this range forms the western wall.

My observation is that the route to liberation lies through self-confidence, not through a list of grievances. If people are confident that they deserve better than what they have been given or are allowed, nothing can stand in their way once they determine to change the world.

At present, virtually every media insists that we pay attention to the minutia of the lives of those who do not engage in productive work—entertainers, professional athletes, politicians—as if these are society's most significant individuals. To affirm instead that the truly significant individuals are those whose labour with brain and body feeds, houses, clothes, heals, educates the community is to me a insurrectionary act. All of us need to be reminded, in the face of the barrage of attention paid to a tiny minority of ridiculously overpaid people, that the work we do each day fabricates the world.

My sense is that most people, given the opportunity, can be highly articulate about what's wrong with how society is presently organized. More complaints about injustice are not likely to be news to them. What keeps people from seeking their own liberation? I think the women's movement, or the fall of the authoritarian state capitalist regimes of Eastern Europe toward the end of the last century, both underscore that the moment people have confidence in their *right* to a better life—feel they are *worth* a better life—society reorganizes itself with remarkable speed.

Do you consider your poems that deal with situations of university life from a professor's perspective to be work poetry?
Yes. A professor is a civil servant, whose salary is paid for from tax dollars. University teaching is organized according to the usual industrial hierarchy, even if in some departments we are allowed to elect our foreperson (a.k.a. department chair), and even comment on who—from a select list—we might best like to be our supervisor (a.k.a. dean). We enjoy some perks like paid sabbaticals that the whole work force would definitely benefit from. But in troubled times, the hierarchy asserts itself and, as is customary in every undemocratic workplace, you accept the idiocy of your "superiors" if you want to keep your job.

In B.C., professors were forbidden by law to organize into unions (just as unions were illegal in most countries at one time or another, and remain so in China and other authoritarian states). Eventually, the faculty at Notre Dame University of Nelson (1950-1977) won union recognition, the first faculty union in the province. B.C. community college faculty were nearly 100 per cent unionized by 1983, and enjoyed on average higher wages and better working conditions than university teachers. However, most college faculty associations saw themselves as groupings of "professionals," rather than union members, until the 1983 public sector general strike. After that experience, the faculty associations accepted the designation of being "locals" of a central union federation.

Since I began to think about work poems, I've always been interested in poetry that encompasses every type of labour: blue- and white-collar, paid and unpaid. Our work writing circle in Vancouver, the Vancouver Industrial Writers' Union (1979-1993), encompassed occupations from doctor to librarian to postsecondary faculty member to carpenter to fisher to railway dining car employee and more.

Did you encounter any difficulties in approaching work writing once you established yourself as a poet?
I've never lived "as a poet"—the pay is pretty lousy. I've always had to have a source of income to live, which usually involves employment.

Along with work, nature seems to be another major subject of your poetry. How do you see the relationship between these two subjects in your writing, since one represents a very human-centred focus and the latter represents a world somewhat beyond human affairs?
Any subject depicted through art involves the human. The activity of art-making is reserved for human beings, for some reason. So art about nature cannot be "beyond human affairs."

Work is central in how we regard nature, just as work is central in every other aspect of our lives. Someone who works in nature—a miner, logger, fisher, farmer, woodlands biologist—sees nature differently than someone to whom nature is a place of respite from work (site of recreation) or than someone who looks with an outsider's eye upon nature as a source of beauty (a beautiful backdrop or contrast to "real" urban life). In the valley in southeastern B.C. where I live when I'm not away working, I have good-sized gardens under cultivation (flowers and veggies). But how I see the wooded slopes around me is quite different from how the mountainside forests are regarded by my neighbours who drive logging truck, or are forestry engineers, or are treeplanters, or who work in one of the local sawmills.

Since your writing often is from an insider's perspective, do you find that the location in which you write influences the subjects you choose to write about (for example city vs. country)?
Since a lot of my poems represent an unfolding autobiography, some experiences and impressions captured in my poems are far more rural after I moved to the country in 1989. Another change in my writing since 1989 is the source of my metaphors and image bank, which have become more organic and less industrial.

*Your approach to poetry runs in opposition to some poetic debate about the starting point for a poem, in that you come to poetry with what seems a fairly conscious goal. From an extreme counter-position, Jack Spicer writes that the poet's motives should be as far removed from the poem as possible (*The House That Jack Built, *5-9). Irving Layton takes a more balanced, middle stance, writing that he is "not much interested in a poet's ideas unless he can make them dance." Since your poems "dance," to use Layton's term, how do you balance your twin interests in making a specific statement, while also writing poems that succeed on an autonomous level?*
Each poem is a complete little universe, and I'd certainly agree with Spicer that sometimes the poem takes over from the writer's intention, and a writer would be foolish to try to force the poem back into complying with her or his original intent. By which I mean that images or ideas can surface in the act of composing a poem that are far more interesting artistically than the content you originally intended the poem to express or the form you intended to employ to convey that content. I try to stay open to the individual poem's autonomy.

Whether a poem "succeeds" or not is a whole other question, though. With music, we're all familiar with songs that either fit our momentary mood or that we're just not in the mood to hear. If I'm not in the mood for reading (or writing) a poem that is difficult of access, does that mean such a poem doesn't succeed?

As with music, a myriad of poetic styles exist. My friend the fabulously ingenious poet Christian Bök, with whom I taught at the University of Calgary, in one essay views poetry as consisting of four discrete games, each with different rules. We might argue about the details of his categories, but I think he's right that you don't criticize Monopoly because it isn't word-based like Scrabble.

The question is whether you regard poetry as a game. Which I don't. Still: "There is room in the jungle," Neruda said in one interview, when the interviewer was trying to goad him into disagreeing with a comment by Jorge Luis Borges, "for both the flea and the elephant." Poetic debates are best conducted within ourselves, according to Neruda. So to me the issue is: what's the ideal poem, in your opinion? At least at this point in your life. How close does the poem you are writing today approach achieving this goal—at least for you?

Do you believe, like some other writers and critics do, that there is a division in Canadian poetry between a more formally experimental style and a more narrative style?

Every poem involves an experiment in form—every artistically conscious poet in every tradition asks himself or herself during the act of composition: "Does this form best convey what I wish the reader to experience?" Every artistically conscious poet tweaks form this way and that during the process of composition to see how form may best serve content.

As commonly used, the tag "experimental poetry" is a coded reference to paratactic writing: poetry that is non-syntactical, often non-narrative or non-referential. As the U.S. poet William Stafford noted in an interview, if an experiment is really being conducted, what is the result? If the word "experiment" means anything, it implies an action whose outcome is capable of being measured. Measurement means a comparison against some scale.

We've had paratactic poetry since at least the Dadaists in 1915. As with the productions of the surrealist movement that followed, the predicted result of these artistic techniques was supposed to be social transformation. "Surrealism, providing dialectic continuity for Dada," wrote J.-M. Monnerot (in *Le Surréalisme au Service de la Révolution*, 1933),

> led poetry to reaches where it no longer belonged to literature. Perched at the extreme limit of the poem, poetry has now only to jump. Even today, its literary form may still be explained by anti-poetic social conditions, which will not ultimately be stamped out until some time after the victory of the communist revolution on a global scale. The surrealists are preparing the ground for the 'transition from quality to quantity' mentioned by [Dada co-founder Tristan] Tzara, for which one of the essential prerequisites is a classless society.

Instead, surrealism has become the favoured technique of television advertising, furthering the goals of capitalist corporations. In any case, no evidence is ever offered that exposure to Dada or surrealist art of any kind leads anyone to adopting a politically revolutionary perspective. As an *experiment*, then, non-syntactical, non-narrative and non-referential writing has been an utter failure. Given this failure, no wonder its present-day practitioners want to keep the sexy label "experimental" but are not interested in talking about the result of the experiment.

If social transformation is not the goal of the experiment, then what is? To "defamiliarize," to "trouble" people's conception of reality—often touted as the reason for creating paratactic writing—are presumably artistic acts undertaken for some *reason,* some end. Otherwise the artist has simply produced gobbledygook. What effect on the reader (if not social transformation, the classic avowed aim) is desired? How could this effect be measured? Does any *evidence* exist that an experiment has succeeded or failed?

Syntactical story-telling, on the other hand, endures both as a means of oppression and of resistance. That is, "narrative" is used by corporations and politicians as a synonym for "spin"—a term meaning at its worst, lying, and at its best, propaganda. Narratives also are how we convey the information we exchange informally with each other to aid our survival in societal hierarchies. Poems I am most interested in fall under the latter category.

In short, I see a division in Canadian poetry between narrative and non-narrative traditions, but not between "experimental" and, presumably, "non-experimental" writing. Formal experimentation, as I say, is a part of every serious compositional approach in every poetic tradition.

If so, how do you see these two divergent styles of writing relating to one another?
Although I agree with Christian that different poets can be seen to be playing by entirely different sets of rules, nevertheless poems are not really just games. Unlike games, literature (what it includes and what it omits) has an effect on social values. I think that poets can learn about writing from exposure to *any* tradition that differs from their own inclination. Classical music has been written based on themes from folk song. We can have acid-jazz-rock fusion in music. I'm always impressed by how open-minded musicians are to diverse influences, compared to poets, who frequently want to close their eyes (and ears) to possibilities from outside their own favoured tradition.

Regarding your poem "In Memory of A.W. Purdy," I would like to ask you a couple of questions about stanza two of the second section. This stanza mentions Purdy's nationalistic sway. How does your conception of Canadian identity differ from Purdy's?
"In Memory of A.W. Purdy" is of course my attempt to rewrite ("write back to," as the postcolonialists would say) Auden's "In Memory of W.B. Yeats." The second section of the latter poem gently critiques some of Yeats' shortcomings (overlooking his writing of patriotic songs for the nascent Irish Fascist movement), while nodding simultaneously

at the shortcomings of poetry and the human landscape. I try to do something similar, except that Purdy communicated such joy about the people and landscapes he encountered that my poem simply can't turn as sour as Auden's ("Intellectual disgrace / Stares from every human face").

However, the "Canadian-ness" of Purdy begs the question I explore in my essay "Laramie or Squamish: What Use is Canadian Culture?", published in my essay collection *A Country Not Considered* (1993). "[*W*]*hich* Canadians are we talking about" when we speak of "Canadian identity"? Or to put the issue another way: "*Whose* Canada do we mean when we speak of Canadian culture?" The essay critiques the obscuring of divergent interests in the name of a spurious national unity.

> [N]ot even colossally expensive public spectacles such as Calgary's 1988 Winter Olympics or Vancouver's Expo 86 can abolish the differences in economic interest between those who are employed for a living and those who employ others for a living. Large taxpayer-funded spectacles are inevitably the occasion for corporate advertisers and public relations experts to generate a great wave of sentimentality about a region or the nation in the hope of motivating sales of various products. But the reality remains that no businessperson would reverse a decision to fire somebody on the grounds that the person affected is an Olympic supporter, or because the man or woman to be fired is a fellow *Albertan* or *Canadian*. Nor would any employer refrain from automating or moving operations to a different part of the world in search of cheaper labor costs on the grounds of patriotism.

Purdy, in my opinion, despite his working-class roots could at times be the poster-boy for the "we're all in this together" mentality. His tremendous affection for life, for people, overshadowed any wish to distinguish competing interests within a vague Canadian whole. He did, however, distinguish between American and Canadian interests. But, again, he saw America as a social monolith, rather than—like the reality of Canada—a complex set of power relations. I try to point this out in the poem by noting that some of the landscapes he loved as Canadian in fact extend intact south of the 49th parallel (or across a different border into Alaska).

You end this stanza with the lines "He called it Canada, but / it was Purdy." In what way do you feel a writer creates his own reality of the world in poetry?
Every poem is to some extent a report from inside an individual consciousness. We merge our own conclusions about the world with our individual command of language and artistic skill, and the poem is the result. So in that sense, just as we live in a specific reality tunnel, so our poems depict something of that tunnel.

My point about Purdy here, though, was more about how his particular vision, as noted in my answer to your preceding question, glosses over social and economic divisions in order to portray a unity that is at best sentimental and at worst politically reactionary. Even if Purdy expressed this view with the best of intentions, and with a lot of humour and fondness!

Do you feel your poetry represents a specifically Canadian perspective?
I believe my poetry represents *a* Canadian perspective, with the emphasis on the article. Given that I was born and have lived most of my life in this country, and given that my poetry is, as I've mentioned, partially an autobiographical project, Canada has to enter into the equation. My poetry definitely doesn't represent *the* Canadian perspective, since I feel such a construct is impossible.

"TO SEE THE TRUTH OF WHAT IS
/ IS TO WANT TO CHANGE IT"

An Interview with Sharon Caseburg
for *Contemporary Verse 2* (2008)

How did your project The Dominion of Love: An Anthology of Canadian Love Poems *(Harbour, 2001) figure into your own writing?*
The project related to my poetry in a couple of ways. First, I'm probably best known for my anthologies of U.S. and Canadian poetry written by people speaking about their own daily work experiences—how their employment affects their lives both on and off the job. I'm talking about my anthologies like *Going For Coffee* (1981) and *Paperwork* (1991) that Harbour published. Although this concern for an insider's work poetry remains very important to me, I'm interested in other kinds of poetry as well. In 1989, for instance, my friend Calvin Wharton and I did an anthology of poems from East Vancouver, *East of Main* (Pulp). Our idea was to demonstrate the incredible breadth and depth of poetry being written in just one part of one Canadian city. The anthology is still the only one ever produced in Canada that includes

lyric and narrative poetry as well as non-representational, non-narrative poetry. Both approaches (really—a myriad of approaches, since each type has dozens of subdivisions) were alive and well in East Van at the time. As luck would have it, we caught the start of the wave of the yuppification of the area, and the book rapidly sold out.

So the love poems project was in part wanting to demonstrate that I had wider interests in poetry than the work writing—although Harbour has kept my work poem anthologies in print. The second way *The Dominion of Love* related to my own writing is that I've always written love poems. My poem "Wayman in Love" is my second-most-reprinted poem, after "Did I Miss Anything?" My second book, *For And Against the Moon* (1974) has probably the most tender sequence I've ever written, called "Living in the Moon." "The Pond" in my 2002 collection *My Father's Cup,* is a love poem which an Edmonton composer, Ryan Purchase, set to music for a chamber ensemble.

How do you approach writing a love poem—happy or sad—without sounding maudlin?

I think ruthless honesty combined with a sense of humour keeps any poem from becoming sentimental. I have a series of poems in *For and Against the Moon* called "The Country of Everyday," and one is written from the viewpoint of a character called The Reality Junkie—a figure I have a lot of admiration for. The Reality Junkie says in the poem: "*To see the truth of what is / is to want to change it.*" In depicting anything on this earth, if you do your job right as an artist you will show the change that is needed. The emotions around love are those of human beings at our rawest. So the need to change the social and economic conditions in which we are trying to construct a decent personality, in which we are trying to love another person and to be worthy of another person's love, is painfully obvious.

But the temptation to simplify—that is, to express things in a false and rosy light, or a mawkish light, or an "emo" light—is very strong because that's much easier than cleaving to a representation of reality that is just as true as you can craft it. So a lot of tension builds up in the process of composition, due to this struggle between a rigorous attention to what is real, and the lure of falsehood. Humour is the tension-breaker, the perspective-granter. The late San Francisco poet Lew Welch (1926-1971) says: "Anyone who confuses his mistress with his muse / is asking for real trouble from both of them." Nowadays we'd phrase this in a more gender-neutral way, but you can see what Welch is getting at.

Do you approach writing love poetry (and all your poetry in general) differently now than you did twenty-five years go?
Definitely my poetry has changed as I've aged. Continually slamming up against a wall in intimate relationships led me to work for a number of years with a counsellor who I found very wise. He helped me see some patterns in my life that are not helpful to me in attaining goals—emotional and otherwise—I set for myself. Various discoveries about the larger patterns of human behaviour, as spelled out in a number of popular books, I've also found very useful. These discoveries have assisted me to understand more about why other people act as they do, as well as why I function as I do. All this has impacted what I pay attention to, and hence what occurs to me as being worth writing about.

Besides differences in content, I like to think that these decades of writing and publishing have kept me changing in other ways as a poet. I don't believe I'm a better writer now—Oscar Wilde famously declared: "Only mediocrities progress." But I think my writing is more conscious of craft than when I began, even as the world has become less vivid to my senses, because life is less fresh to me. On the other hand, I understand an increased amount now about how the world stumbles on another day. Yet I've also become more long-winded: an occupational disease of working for years as a teacher.

Let's talk about rejection—after all, this interview will appear in the "Jilted" issue. You've been fortunate to have a literary career that's spanned more than three decades and spawned more than twenty-five books. At a glance, it doesn't appear as if you've been rejected much. Do you occasionally get rejected, even though you are as well-known as you are? How would you describe your career?

When I first began to send out my poems for publication to literary magazines, I would get rejected about nine times out of every ten submissions. Currently, the rate is about one acceptance out of fifteen or sixteen submissions. And I don't think my writing has gotten worse. But today, decades after I began, far more people are circulating their work for publication. Plus, the advent of the computer has made it easier than ever to submit your poems or stories. Believe me, when each poem or story had to be retyped nearly every time you sent it out, let alone every time you made a slight change in the manuscript, the sheer physical labour and the time involved in preparing manuscripts for submission helped keep down the numbers of people submitting work to magazines. Compounding the problem is that the number of magazines that publish poetry and/or fiction has not grown to keep pace with the exponentially increasing number of potential contributors. So rejection is a central part of the process of being a literary artist today, and I'm no exception.

I taught for some years in the writing program at the Kootenay School of the Arts in Nelson, B.C., and became aware that the situation of constant rejection is identical for a fibre artist or potter. If you take your pottery around from gallery to gallery, whether you're producing sculptural or utilitarian pottery, the response you'll hear is: "Sorry. We already display the work of six potters." Or: "We don't really feel your pottery would be of interest to our clientele." Or: "Your pottery does not meet our present needs." I tell my students that to be a writer, just like to be any kind of artist, means you have to be prepared to step into a river of "No"—a steady stream of "No"s headed toward you. But you'll never reach the island of "Yes" unless you're willing to wade through that water.

I try to make the constant rejection of my work part of my compositional process. If I've submitted a poem or story to a magazine, and it comes back rejected, that writing returns to my house in its *least* favour with me. It's gone out into the world and disgraced itself and come back with its tail between its legs. When I read again what I've written after its failure to be accepted, I have the greatest possible distance from it. On the one hand, it's been gone from my consideration for two months, eight months, or more. As well, it has returned with nothing to show for its travels. When I look at it under these circumstances, I can often see immediately problems with the writing, obvious ways the piece can be improved. Or, I look at it and conclude that it's indeed a work of enduring genius, despite the opinion of the blind fools who have spurned the poem or story. Either way—rewritten once more, or with its laurel re-straightened—the poem or story is sent out another time to seek its fortune.

So I'm grateful to the editors of the literary magazines—often volunteers working long hours at the thankless task of keeping such journals afloat—for helping me refine my writing with their rejections. It's always painful to be rejected, but I take heart from a quote by the U.S. fiction writer Jack London (1876-1916). London says someplace that if he liked a story when he finished writing it, he'd sign it, and send it out for publication. If he didn't like it, he'd sign it, and send it out for publication. I think he had the right idea, as long as you're prepared to be told things like: "Sorry, Tom, not this."

With book manuscripts, as compared to individual poems and stories (or essays, since I also publish those), the situation is much the same. Although my usual poetry publisher, Howard White at Harbour, has been great about steadily publishing collections of my own poems and many of my anthologies, he has to look out for his bottom line and thus only does a set number of literary titles a year. So some ideas I pitch to him are postponed, and some are turned down. My books of fiction each were rejected various places before being accepted.

As I've said, I feel being rejected is inherent in the artistic process— but rejection is a constituent of human relationships in general. It's always a shock when somebody we want to be with doesn't want to be with us. The Russian poet Andrei Voznesensky (1933-2010) has a marvellous poem called "First Ice," about a young woman shivering in a freezing telephone booth being dumped over the phone for the first time. Yet with love, as with literature, you have to be willing to be told "No" if you want to ever hear "Yes." And with love, as with submitting your writing to magazine or book editors, the rejection process is a chance to either improve your product or realize the person you've been dealing with isn't right for what you're offering. Either way, you've benefited from the hurtful event.

In the early years, how difficult was it to get a manuscript published?
When I began to have books of poems published in the 1970s the process was much, much easier than today. Less people were writing poems, books of poems sold in larger numbers than they do now, and publishers were more interested in publishing poetry. At that period in Canada, there was a surge of nationalism that included the idea that the writers of a country are important because their work provides their fellow citizens with a heightened awareness of where they live and how they live, and so potentially contributes to a sense of belonging, of community. The existence of a Canadian literature implies that Canadians might be important, might be worthy of literary attention.

So the media at the time became much more interested in Canadian literature. As the 1970s drew to a close, however, the lords of this life had second thoughts about encouraging nationalism. Economic nationalism requires some national planning, and of course we wouldn't want that—the market must reign over us, free and untrammelled except when it's necessary to have governments pass restrictive labour laws, provide subsidies to select industries, enact tariffs or arrange free-trade deals to protect certain other industries, arrange for resources owned by the commons to become the vehicle for private profit, offer incentives for foreign investment in or foreign ownership of Canadian enterprises, and so on.

Also, nationalism as a movement was too closely linked around the world with socialism. Already in Canada a Council of Canadian Unions had formed of breakaway trade unions, who kept asking why Canada was the only nation in the world whose major unions were controlled from another country. We'd also witnessed how Quebec nationalism was definitely not a good idea as far as the powers-that-be were concerned.

So the media's attention shifted away from the concept of a literary Canada to focus on safer matters. Today the message is that what is important for you to consider is not your life, but either the lives of (mainly U.S.) celebrities or other wealthy people living elsewhere, or those of (mainly U.S.) television characters, i.e., impossible people living nowhere.

The list of Canadian publishers gets shorter every year, with the coup de grace in the past decade being the rise of Chapters-Indigo on the model of the U.S. mega bookstore chains like Borders (some say Chindigo was *designed* to be sold eventually to Borders). Any surviving publisher will talk your ear off as to why Chapters-Indigo threatens the existence of independent Canadian publishing. All a contemporary writer needs to know is that: a) Canadian publishing is still running on the fumes of the nationalist explosion of the 1970s, and b) it becomes harder every year to place a literary title with a Canadian publisher.

You've no doubt seen a lot of love poetry (good and bad) during your career as a creative writing instructor. What advice do you have for your students when it comes to crafting a love poem?
I tell my students to compare the situation of writing work poems and love poems. If you write a poem about a job you have or have had, in many cases you're the first person in the history of the English language to set down in words something about the effects that workplace or occupation has on a human being—at the job, and off the job. Whereas when you write a love poem, you've got at least 500 years of other English-language poets looking over your shoulder—poets who have already expressed a dimension of this emotional state, and who want to make sure you're not just repeating what they've already accomplished.

You better have a unique contribution to make to the topic. It's very nice for you that you're in love—or it's very sad for you that you've been hurt by love—but why should we the readers care? What fresh humour, poignancy, insights into intimate behavioural patterns does your poem offer?

Luckily we have the model of the love *song*. While schlock continues to be churned out by the carload, some songwriters manage to generate invigorating new takes on the age-old subject. Those troubadours

Lyle Lovett and John Hiatt come to mind—say Lovett's "San Antonio Girl" (from *My Baby Don't Tolerate*, 2003):

> San Antonio girl
> She's the one for me
> She ain't exactly white
> But she's a little bit pretty

or Hiatt's fabulous "Trudy and Dave" (from *Slow Turning*, 1990), about a sketchy couple with a baby who "for love" shoot up an ATM to obtain money for the laundromat.

> Well, David put a match to a Lucky Strike
> And smoke curled up 'round his head how he liked.
> It made him feel a little mysterious
> 'Til Trudy said, "David, honey, what about us?"
>
> So he thought about them and those shots ringing out
> And other things he shouldn't be thinking about:
> Like how it wasn't them at all, just life that was mean
> And how a twenty dollar pistol made him feel so clean.
>
> CHORUS: Trudy and Dave,
> They're out of their minds.
> Trudy and Dave,
> They're out of their minds.

The challenge with love poems is to be ruthlessly accurate. The San Francisco poet Lew Welch, whom I mentioned before, claims that we can't hear the world, can't really hear what is said and how people actually speak, because our ears are stuffed with media noise such as lines about love and relationships absorbed from movies, television, or simplistic popular songs. Welch wrote a number of what he called "ear rinses" intended to clean out our hearing to enable us to really *listen*, and thus to be able to capture the power of impassioned speech in our writing. His ear rinses include brief passages that reproduce how people under emotional stress use language: a frustrated man calling a cat that won't respond, or a couple arguing about who is to blame after a camera is stolen from their parked car. Accuracy, expressed through language that is at least as powerful as the words ordinary people actually use under positive or negative stress, seems to me the key to writing good love poems—or any good poems.

What advice do you have regarding writing poetry in general?
I'll say this:

1. Nobody in the history of the human race has had your experiences. If you don't write what it is like for you to live in your time, in your place, somebody else will do it for you and get it wrong.

2. Musicians and wannabe musicians listen to music *all* the time, seeing what riffs to emulate, steal and avoid. These people buy or otherwise acquire recordings endlessly, and are forever going to clubs and concerts to observe and listen. Artists and wannabe artists of every type (painting, clay, fine woodworking, etc.) look at examples of their art *all* the time, going to galleries and artist's talks, and looking at photos in exhibit catalogues and books. Journeyed tradesmen and tradeswomen *constantly* observe how other craftspeople practice their trade, again looking for ideas to adapt, avoid or adopt. As Lew Welch says in his poem "Philosophy" from *Course College* (1968): "The great Winemaster is almost a / magician to the bulk of his Tribe, / to his Peers he is only accurate." You need to steadily read other people's poems in literary magazines, individual volumes, and selected and collected works.

You need to be reading poems *all* the time, the way a superb ball player is forever noodling around with a ball, or a great guitarist is forever noodling around with her or his instrument.

3. Quit whining. Nobody asked you to be an artist. Nobody promised that your poems would dazzle the ages, let alone your fellow-citizens or fellow-writers. Nothing entitles you to a grant or award, or to publication in a literary magazine, inclusion in an anthology, or the acceptance of your manuscript by a publisher. Yes, people with less talent than you will be hailed as stunning practitioners of your art. Yes,

some people are luckier than you. Your most effective response to the crooked hand fate has dealt you—or will deal you—is to keep writing. Writing well is not the best revenge, it is the only revenge. External validation is notoriously fickle, as well as notoriously wrong-headed.

On this last point, when I teach a senior poetry workshop I assign the most insightful book I've ever encountered about the artistic life, *The Horse's Mouth* (1944) by Joyce Cary (1888-1957). Cary's central character, Gulley Jimson, is a William-Blake-obsessed painter down on his luck, but with his creative powers intact despite his poverty, approaching old age, and nearly universal critical neglect. How Jimson negotiates his situation is both hilarious and offers a much better model for the artistic process than I could formulate. Indeed, laughter is probably the most useful advice anyone can offer you, if you know how to take it. The U.S. poet and teacher Philip Levine (1928-2015) was a contemporary literary figure so revered he's the only writer I've ever seen get a standing ovation from a huge crowd (at the Associated Writing Programs conference in Palm Springs in 2001) *before* he started to read. One of his former students explained to me: "Phil helped us to take our poems seriously when we didn't, and helped us *not* take our poems so seriously when we did."

THE SIXTIES WERE ABOUT HOPE: WOODSTOCK RISING

An Interview with Clelia Scala
for "Open Book Toronto" (May 2010)

Tell us about your novel, Woodstock Rising.

The 1960s continue to cast a huge shadow forward into our life today. Socially, politically, culturally we're still processing all that those brief years initiated. Geoffrey O'Brien, in his book *Dream Time: Chapters from the Sixties* (Counterpoint, 1988), at one point calls the era a renaissance. I think that's true: the Renaissance in Europe in the fourteenth to seventeenth centuries was a time when everything changed socially, politically, culturally. No time period after the European Renaissance radiated the same magic until the explosion of light, colour, creativity and change of the Sixties. The multifaceted legacy of that time continues to suffuse our lives.

I had wanted to write a book about the 1960s that shows how all the changes that we've come to identify as representative of those years were occurring simultaneously, each influencing the others. Most accounts of the Sixties I've read single out only one subject—rock music, or radical politics, or the counter-culture—whereas none of these really occurred in isolation from each other. And all of these changes happened amid the usual concerns of young people: school/career/dating and mating.

Woodstock Rising traces the lives of a group of young men and women—one of them Canadian—in the beach cities of southern California through the tumultuous fall, winter and spring of 1969-1970, following the Woodstock Festival in August 1969. The core time-line of the book is the actual occurrences that marked the months that the novel spans. But in order to accurately convey the uncertainties that were part of the feeling of being young in those days, the characters are also involved in a fictional event that *could* have happened but didn't.

Did you have a specific readership in mind when you wrote your book?
I had two different audiences in mind. One is young people active today in organizations dedicated to social change, whether environmental or anti-globalization. In the Sixties, because of the fear of McCarthyism, people who had fought in the social struggles of the 1930s did not speak up about what they had learned through their experiences. This meant many of us active in the movements for social change in the 1960s had to re-invent the wheel and committed errors that might otherwise have been prevented. I wanted to pass along specifically what happened in the late Sixties when an attempt was made to fast-track the adoption by the student movement of a rigid ideology. Up until then, even radical student organizations in practice had functioned as loose coalitions. The *intent* of becoming more doctrinaire was to make the student movement more effective as an agent for social change. But imposing a specific ideology had the opposite effect.

The second audience for *Woodstock Rising* is the minority of men and women who participated in the activities by which the Sixties are now known. Though lots of silliness occurred, and some awful things happened (which also appear in the novel), by and large those who embraced the changes were right to do so, and deserve praise. The Woodstock Festival was so significant because it was the first time that those of us who embodied what have come to be regarded as Sixties values felt we weren't a tiny minority in our society. My novel stresses that most people went through the Sixties as though they were living in the Fifties, which is why I bridle when people talk about boomers "selling out." The majority of my peers never bought in—they turned up their nose at what was exciting when they were young, and missed much of what later everybody recognized as sparking all the significant changes that have so influenced the subsequent years. People I know who back then held the values we regard as Sixties values haven't wavered in their beliefs. The conformists and go-along types back then also haven't changed much either.

When people jeer at the Sixties, mostly because such mockers are made uneasy by the values the minority in that era championed, people invariably mention "sex, drugs and rock and roll." All these actually happened, and appear in my novel, but really the list is: "sex, drugs, rock and roll, and *politics*"—and the last term greatly influenced the other three. Young people were at the forefront of the civil rights movement protesting racism and segregation, at the forefront of the women's movement, and at the forefront of the anti-draft movement, the anti-Vietnam War movement, and the anti-imperialist movement. Eventually, some young people realized that protest was not enough— that what was needed was a fundamental rethinking about alternative ways to organize a self-governing society.

In my view, the main characteristic for which the Sixties can't be forgiven is that it presented the possibility of creating a better world in which everyday life would be more *fun* for everybody. Most models for social change before or since—whether authoritarian communism or the unbridled free market—offer a dour world of winners and losers. Today's environmentalists dream a world in which you're morally more pure, but have to make do with less, put up with discomfort in support of noble aims. The Sixties said, in the words of the slogans of the 1968 Paris May Days revolt that united students with radical workers: "The more I make love, the more I want to make the revolution" and "Live without dead time." My favourite saying from those days is: "Under the pavement, the beach."

What was the inspiration for Woodstock Rising?
I've felt sickened by Canada's armed participation in a hopeless and brutal war in Asia, propping up a corrupt narco-administration that wouldn't last forty-eight hours without an ever-increasing supply of foreign troops. Opposing the consortium of druglords and warlords in Kabul is a Pashtun tribal movement of religious psychopaths, women-fearing and women-hating, who are equally involved in the drug trade that continues to have such an awful impact on our inner cities. The latter murderous bunch are the ones "our" side armed and trained when the religious nutters agreed to fight the *previous* group of foreign invaders who propped up a puppet corrupt narco-administration.

The parallels between our intervention in an Afghan civil war and America's war in Asia forty years ago are too many to list, but at least at that time a vocal and active minority on the campuses organized—together with groups in the wider community—to oppose the conflict. The time seemed right to me to draw those parallels, although *Woodstock Rising* eschews irony: the reader has to make the connections, and the novel uses humour as well as outrage to put across its ideas.

As a university teacher I've also been bothered by how much my students lack hope: they see no real alternative to the corporate state in which they were raised. The limits of their imagination about social change is to click a button on some online petition, or recycle their used paper, or purchase some upgrade or techno-device whose sellers insist will improve their lives.

Most of all, the Sixties were about hope. So much had changed so fast that we who were socially active in that period believed we could change *everything* for the better. That sense of hope gave us energy to build new institutions. As just one example, most of the independent Canadian publishers still around started in the brief wave of Sixties enthusiasm for having an independent country: Harbour, Talonbooks, Anansi, Coach House, etc. People organized the Council of Canadian Unions, finally tiring of being the only nation on earth whose unions were headquartered in a different country. Every social institution—from schools to marriages—was up for reconsideration. In fashion, we went from drab conformity and rigid dress codes to a virtual rainbow of color, shape, form. Compare a street scene in 1962 to one in 1972 and you'll see what I mean. About the only fashion innovation since the Sixties is the discovery that a person can wear a baseball cap backwards.

By now it's a truism that "social media" isolates people, rather than unites them in any meaningful way. An article in the June 1, 2009 *Maclean's* discusses Ang Lee's new movie *Taking Woodstock*. Ang Lee turns a social marker into a gay coming-of-age story, which it most certainly wasn't. But that's not what's significant about the *Maclean's* piece. Rather, it talks about how the young stars of the film recognize that the electronic devices they embrace actually encourage conformity and lack of fun. "If you were a 23-year-old guy in Woodstock and didn't have a phone, you were just hanging out," one actor is quoted. "Whoever you were with, that's who you were with. These days you're with who you're with plus the ten people you're text-messaging." Another actor notes the absence back then of cell phone cameras and the ability to immediately post photos and videos to websites. The implication is that the ever-present electronic eye is a huge inhibiter of spontaneity, of natural behaviour, of concern for others. "You wonder if [Woodstock] were happening today what it would be like," the actor says. "Would people be able to go beyond themselves and care about something bigger?"

Did you draw on people you know for your characters?
Absolutely. Some characters in *Woodstock Rising* are actual historical figures like Richard Nixon. Other characters are composites based on politicos or freaks or ordinary students I knew from the time-period of the book.

When did you first try writing, and what did you write?
I had always been "good at English," since my parents were readers. My grade seven English teacher in Prince Rupert, B.C., Ray Logie—later

named the B.C. provincial animator for drama—thought I could adapt for the stage the opening scenes of Robert Louis Stevenson's *Treasure Island*, and I did. Mr. Logie organized a stage production of this adaptation, which was quite a thrill for me. Later, like most young people, I began writing in high school out of that adolescent turmoil that claims us all. I was lucky in that I grew up in a household that contained the latest books by contemporary Canadian poets, so I turned to poetry. I also somehow read Lawrence Lipton's *The Holy Barbarians* (1959), about beatniks living in Venice, California (a suburb of Los Angeles), and that book included examples of beat poetry, whose loose forms were ideal for expressing adolescent angst.

What's the best advice you've ever received as a writer?
To read. Constantly. But not to read as a civilian does, mentally inhaling the words. To read as a writer does: why doesn't this paragraph work? Why am I bored here? Why do these characters seem rounded, engaging—*how* does the author make me care about what happens to these people?

WRITING FROM THE EDGES

An Interview with Diane Guichon
for *The Writer's Chronicle* (2009)

Tom, students learning the craft of poetry writing are often interested in understanding the poetic practices of other poets. What is your writing process?
I need to have a clear period of time and a quiet space in which to work. So I wouldn't write, for example, in my office at the University of Calgary. But I had no problem working in my Calgary home office (at least before the tasks of reading student writing, and marking essays and other assignments piled up too high each term). Mostly I write in the basement study of my home in B.C. I don't use writing journals but tend to jot down on odd slips of paper brief notes about a subject or object that has evoked in me either an emotion or observation that I feel deserves to be developed into a poem. When I have time, I return to these notes and attempt to craft a poem from them. I usually produce a first draft in longhand, and then move to the computer. Maybe my writing process has something to do with my background in journalism, since I start with handwritten notes that are expanded, eventually, into a finished piece of writing.

How much time do you spend editing your work?

I spend an *enormous* amount of time editing. I think of my poems as scores for oral recitation, so I go over them and over them until I'm satisfied with how they feel and sound. As a writer I'm always questioning whether a poem of mine is completed. I use the process of sending poems I've decided are done to literary magazines to obtain space for myself to try to see a drafted poem objectively. Sometimes when a poem I submit to a literary magazine is accepted by one of the first journals I try, I start second-guessing myself and wondering if something is wrong with the poem since it was accepted so readily. More usually, rejections from magazines allow me critical distance to revaluate a poem and see its faults more clearly. Or on rereading it, I conclude that, no, these editors are idiots: this poem *is* a dazzling work of literary splendour. Either way, revised or not, the rejected piece goes back in the mail as soon as possible.

Do you deal with mostly one editor or one press or submit your work to various presses depending on the project?

My work has been published by a wide variety of publishers over the years, including McClelland & Stewart, the old Macmillan of Canada, Anansi in Toronto, plus prairie publishers like Thistledown and Turnstone, and of course Harbour in B.C. Two books of my poems have been published by Ontario Review Press, who, despite the name, were located in Princeton, New Jersey. I probably have the longest association with Harbour, who operate from the Sunshine Coast north of Vancouver. Howard White, Harbour's owner and publisher, is a friend and we've developed a good relationship over the years. I also submit individual poems to many different literary magazines, i.e. *Hudson Review, New Quarterly, Event*. I tend to submit repeatedly to certain magazines if they from time to time accept something of mine, until the editors change and the magazine is no longer interested in my work at all.

You have been engaged in writing and publishing poetry for decades. How have your poetic practices changed over time?

My process of writing has stayed pretty much constant, but perhaps the audience has changed. When I create, as I mentioned, I write from that kernel of an idea or emotion that sparks the poem for me. That practice hasn't changed. My style of writing, too, has remained essentially the same: free verse, with line and stanza breaks providing rhythmic cues, and the tone conversational but employing figurative language including frequent elaborate development of metaphors.

Of course, I've learned certain things from my writing students over the years. For instance, I had a student who flatly refused to read anybody's poem that was just one big stanza: a tower poem. That student demanded more variety in a poem's appearance on the page, and I think she had a point—although I wouldn't take quite so absolute a position as she did. And I've learned lots to emulate and to avoid by reading published poets, from approaches to various subjects—for example, ways of expressing one's interactions with the natural world—to aspects of craft—for example, how does a poem in the form of a series of two-line stanzas differ in feeling from a poem written in three-line stanzas?

When I write, though, I see a physical audience in front of me, listening to me read the poem. I write to what I think the audience can take in, respond to. What has changed dramatically over the years is the attitude of the audience *toward* poetry. When I began to write, prevailing social and artistic views meant that Canadian poetry was regarded as a significant art form. This was back in the late 1960s and early Seventies. Today, poetry is as vibrant an art form as ever—maybe more energetic now than ever before. But poems are off the cultural radar nearly completely. Poetry certainly is not seen as having anything to contribute to a sense of how Canadians—or Americans, for that matter—view themselves as a community, a people, a nation. I watched poems make a definite contribution to the anti-Vietnam War movement, the black power movement, the women's movement, and Canadian nationalism. Yet the art form at the moment is not where many people look for news—oppositional or otherwise—about their world.

So the current audience for poetry always seems to me a little shamefaced. People at readings, no matter how raucous, or people buying a poetry book are aware that they are celebrating an art form that the surrounding culture does not validate in any significant way.

You have been criticized by Carmine Starnino most recently for "flatly pro-saic" poetry. He has said that "maybe at some point in the game Wayman's dedication to lack-of-artifice was a liberating force, but at this stage, however, it is a curiously depressing refusal of everything that is mysterious and shaking and renewing in poetry." With the poets of The New Canon *Starnino believes that he has gathered together examples of writing from a new generation of poets such as Diana Brebner and Bruce Taylor who demonstrate a "vigorous reinvestment in verbal resources which were stifled in the seventies and eighties; poems that live inside their linguistic action, for whom language is so important it gets the whole of their attention." Starnino's approach to poetry reminds me of the purist stand of the New Critics who looked to poems as stand-alone works of art reflecting a more complicated sequence of language or form that required attention and interpretation to fully understand. It would seem Starnino sees little poetry in your poems.*

In the Chilean poet Pablo Neruda's 1971 Nobel lecture, "Toward the Splendid City," he says (in the Nobel Foundation's translation):

> The truth is that, even if some or many consider me to be sectarian, barred from taking a place at the common table of friendship and responsibility, I do not wish to defend myself, for I believe that neither accusation nor defense is among the tasks of the poet. When all is said, there is no individual poet who administers poetry, and if a poet sets himself up to accuse his fellows, or if some other poet wastes his life in defending himself against reasonable or unreasonable charges, it is my conviction that only vanity can so mislead us.

In the Nobel lecture Neruda goes on to state that "the enemies of poetry are to be found not among those who practice poetry or guard it." In another interview he states that the real enemies of poetry are those who drop bombs on children. I'd expand that to say that the enemies of poetry are those forces of greed and violence that periodically overtake individuals, nations, religions, organizations or communities.

Inevitably, people under the sway of these forces are led to deny the humanity of fellow members of our struggling species.

I see poetry as a tool useful for beneficial social ends. A good, useful tool can be beautiful or ugly, obvious or ingenious, common or hard to obtain. What's more, people are constantly inventing new excellent tools, even though some of our most enduringly useful tools are thousands of years old. The new doesn't always improve, invalidate or supplant the old, despite the enthusiasm of some innovators.

Of course, Oscar Wilde famously said that all art is quite useless. But people have found Wilde's pithy sayings—his artistry with words—of enormous use: for instance, Wilde's humour induces people to encounter, and thus possibly consider, contrarian perceptions about the world.

You quote Pablo Neruda in your last answer. Elsewhere you have written of his influence on your work. What other poets have influenced your writing? Of those poets writing today, whose work do you admire?
Among Canadian poets I've been greatly influenced by Al Purdy for his mastery of the anecdotal and conversational, for his achievement of a transparency of craft. I have found inspiration in Spanish-language poetry in translation, particularly a range of poetries arising out of Latin America. In the U.S., poets such as Kenneth Rexroth, Theodore Roethke, Denise Levertov, Marge Piercy, Robert Bly, Gary Snyder, Philip Levine, Billy Collins taught me much. I have an ongoing dialogue about writing that is vital to me with a UC Irvine classmate and close friend, the California poet Dennis Saleh. My writing has been influenced by 1960s rock lyrics, and such folk lyricists as Phil Ochs, Tim Hardin, Bob Dylan. More latterly the lyricists Bruce Hornsby, Stan Ridgway, John Hiatt, James Keelaghan, Among contemporary work poets, I've learned from and enjoy the writing of Clem Starck, Jim Daniels, Kate Braid, Susan Eisenberg, as well as others.

The cover art for many of your books of poetry such as Free Time, A Planet Mostly Sea, *and* Money and Rain, *among others, is simply a photograph of Tom Wayman. This links the image of Tom Wayman directly to the poetry inside the covers. This link is also accentuated by your habit of referring to yourself in third person as "Wayman." How different is the poet Tom Wayman from the man Tom Wayman? Do you know of any other poet who markets his image in a similar fashion? Could not a student analyze your work from the theoretical perspective that your poems reflect a long series of representations that might very well be fictional?*

Well, when I started out publishing my poems, the book covers were simply meant to correspond to the cover art on many folk music albums.

Here I was trying to make a connection between the cover and the subject matter in the poems and instead the covers link your work to folk ballads. That would seem to reinforce the concept you mentioned earlier about your poems as scores for oral recitation.

The album covers of folk artists recording in the Sixties and Seventies often projected a particular image of the musician. You can chronicle, for example, Bob Dylan's changing sense of who he wanted to be by how he appears on his covers: contrast "Self Portrait" or "Nashville Skyline" with "Hard Rain" or "Street Legal."

The "Wayman" poems I wrote for many years arose because of a wish to avoid the endless repetition of the lyrical "I". When I changed the "I" in the poems to the third person "Wayman," I also discovered more potential for humour. So drafts of "I" poems that were moaners and groaners would transmute to comic "Wayman" poems. I originally got the idea from a poem by Philip Levine called "Looking for Levine." The poem, about Levine's search for his North African ancestry, isn't funny. But "Looking for Levine" was the inspiration for me to write "Waiting for Wayman," the first of a too-long series of this kind of poem I churned out for decades.

As for the cover art's relation to the poetic representation between the book covers, of course the Wayman (or an "I") in the poetry is different from who I am as a person. The written word is always a photograph—a cropped photograph, at that. Anybody's life consists of constant change until death; a poem abstracts an instant or hour or day out of a seamless flow. So my personality—with all its quirks, flaws, baggage, and, I hope, a few positive qualities—is far more complex than the "Wayman" personae or an "I" allows. Huge aspects of my life never make it into my poems; yet some of my poems are as autobiographical as my particular use of the genre permits. But the person in the poems as a whole—or the cover art!—is not the real me. For one thing, people who meet me after having first read my poems often blurt out: "You're a lot smaller than I thought you'd be."

Alan Soldofsky in the summer 2006 edition of The Writer's Chronicle, *in an article entitled "The Lyric Self: Artifice and Authenticity in Recent American Poetry," places the Post-Confessional poetry of the last thirty-odd years within a tradition of poetry writing dating back to Coleridge and Wordsworth. Your work would seem to fall within this category. He discusses the building of a lyric self, one grounded in a particular locale and imbued with a certain sincerity of voice and intimacy with the reader. He points to the fact that sometimes this becomes a "confidence game" and involves the reader in a contrived fiction. Any comments?*

I very much like the article you mention, and have used it in my teaching. Yet I think the lyric self goes back much further than the Romantics. Think of the folk ballad lyric "I" with its roots in pre-Elizabethan times. Also, the process of representation *inherently* involves a fiction. Even in the documentary form, material is edited, omitted, shaped for artistic effect. A poem of mine may be based on my sense of reality. But as my writing takes the form I call a poem, reality is necessarily reconstructed.

We see an "I" fictionalized for effect in anybody's daily storytelling. "My Dad will kill me," a young person says. That mortal danger isn't real, although that's how a young person convincingly communicates her or his assessment of an emotionally threatening situation. When I drive through the mountains near my home in southeastern B.C., a deer or other large animal frequently darts in front of my truck—over the years, I've hit and killed a deer and winged an elk. To describe a close encounter, I might say: "I missed that deer by *inches.*" The reality is, perhaps, the deer dashed in front of the vehicle *nine feet* ahead of my rapidly approaching bumper. To convey to you how the experience felt, I have to say "inches." It's a fiction, but a necessary part of effective storytelling. You might say that "inches" is an accurate fiction, whereas "nine feet" is the literal truth. Accurate fiction that conveys the sincerity and intimacy that Soldofsky speaks of, that communicates a self's experiences to other people, is probably as ancient as the first cave dwellers' campfire tales about the day's events.

Perhaps this has something to do with propaganda, but could you address the issue concerning the various leftist organizations or movements you have belonged to over the years such as the anti-Vietnam War movement in the late Sixties in California and Colorado, the Students for a Democratic Society, the "Wobblies"—Industrial Workers of the World—and Operation Solidarity in B.C., the public sector general strike in 1983 which protested the provincial government's cutbacks to social programs. Has time, age, or experience changed your political interests?

I have a problem with your description of these organizations as "left," although I'm aware that is frequently the tag placed on such movements. Once they are labelled as "left," instantly some people stop thinking about them—pro or con. In fact, all these forms of social activism I was involved in were broad coalitions, uniting as many people as possible around certain social goals, whether or not adherents of these goals believed in Marx or in alien abduction or that milk is bad for you. Part of the anti-Vietnam War movement, for example, was resistance to military conscription. In southern California, the Santa Ana *Register*—an otherwise very right-wing newspaper—supported the Vietnam War editorially as an anti-Communist crusade, but opposed the draft as un-American involuntary servitude. No one would have called the *Register* "left-wing" for opposing the draft.

To allow the Vietnamese people to determine their own destiny—as they had been trying to do ever since the Japanese occupation ended—was no threat to the security of the United States, even if the Vietnamese chose to support a Communist government. Indeed, this lack of a threat was proven after the U.S. lost the war and was driven from the country. All that killing and maiming of people and destruction of human hope and potential, all the trashing of the environment, values and ethics, was for nothing. Life in the U.S. for the overwhelming majority of citizens went on exactly as previously. Even before the U.S. was defeated, a huge spectrum of people could see that the Vietnam War and its accompanying military draft was a pointless expenditure of human lives and money. Genuine leftists were part of that coalition, yes, but also people from an astonishing number of backgrounds and political persuasions.

Similarly, S.D.S.' opposition to war, imperialism, racism, and corporate control of daily life—and how the educational system fosters these malevolences—involved young people who held a wide range of views. The I.W.W., as a working class organization, has always known that *many* solutions to a social problem are possible—just as on the job a task can be accomplished in more ways than the boss or Standard Operating Procedure or the union contract dictates. That diversity of opinions and skills—while striving for identifiable, common goals—is the strength of a coalition. Variety can make for a more fractious organization, but monolithic structures of either the right or left have not fared well in the past 100 years. Operation Solidarity arose from a non-political idea—to resist a provincial budget based on the curtailment of social services and a public sector wage freeze. Police officers' wages were frozen under the new budget legislation, along with other public sector workers, and the police union participated in some protest activities. Despite how the media and government may have tagged Operation Solidarity, I doubt the police saw themselves as "leftists."

In Operation Solidarity's public sector general strike, we were looking to see what we had in common with others, how to improve everyday living conditions for as many of us as possible. It's no secret that the way people live and work is different from society's official definitions, or at least what gets pitched back to us by governments and media. Daily work is where we reproduce society every day—not just the goods and services we all depend on, but the power relations that currently control how a society functions and what goods and services will be available to us. My writing has been involved in articulating the material living conditions that get reproduced every day at our jobs. Such writing is one place where my political practice is engaged.

About the only way I can see my political beliefs having changed is an increased appreciation of the concept of a politics without enemies. I can oppose your ideas, your actions, without making you into a demon, into a less-than-human entity. Take away the power of Lyndon B. Johnson or George W. Bush or Stephen Harper to diminish human enjoyment of this planet, and these men appear as awfully sad human beings. Our task, then, is end their power to hurt, maim, kill, destroy. We don't need to categorize them as devils from Hell or invaders from Planet X in order to oppose them. That tribal urge to classify as subhuman anyone who differs from me, who does not think as I do, is hard to limit. Once I identify X and Y as non-human, pretty soon I'm accusing others on my own side of being traitors, betrayers, of being something evil that needs to be cast out or exterminated. Such behaviour is a slippery slope that we don't have to go down to win a better world.

The dominant voice in poetry in Canada today seems to belong to the avant-garde or the experimental poet. In the summer 2006 edition of The Writer's Chronicle, *D. W. Fenza, in an article, "The Words and the Bees," goes so far as to suggest that the decline of the English major and audiences for literature might be attributed to the Language poets as "they have tortured our poor mother tongue." Fenza states that the writer's chief task is "humble, elusive, and hard: the accurate description of our society." Do you agree?*
I'd have to disagree with you that the dominant poetic voice is non-representational. If you survey the style of poetry published most often by the majority of literary journals and literary presses, the mainstream is obviously free-verse, narrative, lyric. The Calgary literary scene might give you the sense that paratactic writing is dominant in Canadian poetry because of a very active group of poets that happen to live and write in Calgary. But, as I say, any sort of objective overall assessment of literary magazines and poetry publishers will reveal such writers as a noisy, but rather minor, aspect of current literary activity.

As for Fenza's comments, I suspect there are a lot of reasons why audiences for literature have declined. Each of us today face a stultifying barrage of media attempting to convince you that certain individuals are the truly significant figures of our society. These are people whose contribution, we're repeatedly told, far outweighs that of those whose work feeds, clothes, houses, heals and educates us, and allows us opportunity for travel, recreation, and amusements other than those conveyed on a screen or via an earbud. A convergence of interests are glad if you are not paying attention to the significance of your own life—one of literature's major strengths—but to the airbrushed versions of the lives of a handful of celebrity figures. I don't believe there is much point in demonizing Language poets as responsible for a lack of serious readers. All of us have sinned. Creative writing courses have been taught at the postsecondary level since 1945 in an ever-increasing number of institutions. Hundreds of creative writing MFA and MA programs operate in North America, for instance. Yet sales of poetry books are going down, not up. Literary magazines have pathetic circulation numbers. Why did we fail to make readers of more of our students, even as we helped them become writers?

You mentioned to me once that at a reading at a literary conference in Calgary a group of experimental poets walked out of the room when a "traditional" or "lyric" poet began reading. What do you think is wrong with the community of Canadian poets today?
I think there is a failure to acknowledge variant approaches to an art form that is in fact very broad in its sweep—spoken word, lyric, narrative, non-narrative, and so on. Of course, young people are far more judgmental in their attitudes than we veterans. When you practice an art for a long time, you get a sense that you can learn from many different schools, that your own artistic practice still has room to grow, to improve. Writing for years in Vancouver—a city known for its literary gangs and literary muggings—I remember myself and my friends dismissing adherents of one style of non-representational writing as "toque, scarf and handbag poets," due to the particular uniform they adopted for readings. Later on, we discovered we had far more in common with these people—as faculty colleagues in the B.C. community college system, and as long-time practitioners of the literary arts—than we had differences. We got to quite like, even admire, them.

I never hear musicians publicly denouncing other musicians who are inspired by different traditions or developments. Instead, musicians *listen*: maybe there's something here I can incorporate into my work. People have told me that's because music is a more collective art form than writing, that writing attracts loners, egos that can't stand competition or approaches that differ from or even contradict their own. I like to think poets are more broad-minded than that.

Any subject seems capable of being turned into a poem by Tom Wayman. You write poems about correcting papers, interstates, jobs you've held, people you've met, sex, etc. What subjects would you say you have you not written about?
I'm a person who has lived more on the edges than at the centre.

What do you mean by that?
This insight came when I was working with a counsellor a number of years ago. He helped me see that in many areas of my life I had chosen the periphery and not the centre. For instance, I've taught mainly for community colleges and alternative postsecondary institutions, rather than at universities. I've been more active in the radical fringe of the labour movement than in mainstream unions. My writing has mainly been in poetry, not prose. In relationships with others—intimate and otherwise—my tendency for much of my life also has been to hang back, not step forward into full commitments. Somehow, being on the edges feels emotionally safest for me. I have sensed some risk involved with moving to occupy the centre. My avoidance of those risks carries into the poems.

It has been eighteen years since you wrote about the importance of articulating the workplace in "Visible Consequences, Invisible Jobs" in your Introduction to Paperwork *(1991). Depictions of daily work are still predominantly absent from contemporary Canadian writing, both in poetry and fiction. How do you feel about that?*
As I've written in a number of essays: since work is central to human experience, an accurate depiction of daily work can't be kept forever

from assuming a central place in art, including literature. Work poetry has never died, even though some work writing groups that flourished in the closing decades of the last century—like the Vancouver Industrial Writers' Union, which I helped found, or the San Francisco Waterfront Writers and Artists—have disbanded. Yet fisher poets currently gather each winter in Astoria, Oregon, organized by Jon Broderick and others, and have produced several anthologies. I recently received a wonderful manuscript of poems by a woman about her job working in the Alberta oil patch. A fellow in Ottawa with tremendous energy organized a national competition for work poems, the judges for which included the head of the Canadian Autoworkers union. Sue Doro's *Pride and a Paycheck* newsletter from Oakland, California for tradeswomen often features poems by them. In Plano, Texas, David LaBounty's Blue Cubicle Press has published since 2005 a series of occupational anthologies (*Tales from the Cubicle*, *Tales from the Classroom*, *Tales from the Clinic*) and individual work-based fiction chapbooks under the Workers Write! imprint.

Still, you can pick up literary anthology after anthology that presents a portrait of a country in which nobody works. You can attend reading after reading at most literary festivals and never know that the central and governing experience of most human beings' lives is the job they have or want. Leaf through most high school English textbooks and note how many of the poems or stories included deal with how our employment affects our lives on and off the job. By omitting an accurate depiction of daily work, literature in effect says that work has no value—just as once the omission of women's experiences from literature in effect proclaimed that women's experiences had no value. This absurd situation won't continue forever, and I'm proud of having helped chip away at the stone wall blocking the honest expression of the ways in which our employment shapes the quality of our lives.

What kind of poetry, in what form or on what subjects, do you think you would write if you were a 22-year-old English graduate student today? What a great question! I'd have to say I absolutely don't know. I came to poetry during the Sixties when everything was up for reconsideration:

the role of each societal institution, the way you dressed, what music you listened to, the best means to effect social change, how to live in harmony with the biosphere, and more. We were confident in our ability to solve the problems that faced us, and to have a rocking good time while we overcame every obstacle. That optimism about life and the possibilities for change, and about our efficacy as individuals and collectively, is definitely not the possession of the 22-year-olds I meet. Since I have no real sense of how they comprehend the world into which they have just emerged as adults, I can't imagine what they would write about it. Which is why I read what they *do* write with intense interest.

What do you see as the future for poetry in Canada?
I see a potentially rich future. Poets might yet acknowledge that the present wide diversity of approaches to their art is a source of strength, rather than conflict. Perhaps we could experience as a result a surge in creativity, a forward-looking artistic development that restores greater popularity to the art. In any case, the pendulum of attention may well swing. If you marginalize something long enough, after a while people ask: "Hey, what's going on over there? Why are we expected to ignore that? Maybe they're having more fun over there than we are here." We're a species with a lot of curiosity. One friend of mine, the poet, fiction writer, and musician John Lent, observes that jazz historically has fallen in and out of fashion, in and out of cultural significance. He says: "Why not poetry?"

ACKNOWLEDGEMENTS

Many thanks to the editors and staffs of the publications in which components of this book first appeared, often in earlier forms.

The poem "If You're Not Free at Work, Where Are You Free?" is from my collection *Dirty Snow* (2012) and is reprinted by permission of Harbour Publishing Co. Ltd. First published in *The Capilano Review* 3.3 (Fall 2007).

The interview "Affirmative Poetry" was published in a shorter version entitled "The Real Planet" in *Acta Victoriana* 134.1 (2009-2010).

"Against the Smiling Bastards" was published in *The New Quarterly* 101 (Winter 2007).

"Avant-Garde or Lost Platoon? Postmodernism as Social Control" was published in *Canadian Poetry* 76 (Spring/Summer 2015).

"The Bloodhound and the Skein: On Narrative in Poetry" was published in *The New Quarterly* 17.3 (1997).

"Every Page" was published in *Ne West Review* 26.3/4 (2001). The essay is based on a talk given Feb. 1, 2001 at Green College, University of B.C., as part of a symposium on "The State of Work Writing: A Postmortem on the Vancouver Industrial Writers' Union (1979-1993)" organized by the College's speakers' committee in conjunction with the Labour Studies program at Simon Fraser University.

I Can Feel the Future Trembling: Official Dreams, Dreams of Work" was published in a slightly shorter version in *Canadian Dimension* 31.3 (May-June 1997).

"Love's Provinces and Territories" is the introduction to my *The Dominion of Love: An Anthology of Canadian Love Poems* (Madeira Park, BC: Harbour, 2001).

"Paddling Toward a Better World: On George Hitchcock (1914-2010) and *Kayak* (1964-1984)" appeared in *Caliban online* 3 (2011) under "Contributors' Advice."

The interview "The Sixties Were About Hope" appears in a longer version on Open Book Toronto's website (www.openbooktoronto.com/news/writing_with_tom_wayman; starting May 20, 2010) entitled "On Writing, With Tom Wayman."

"To Be Free Full-Time: The Challenge of Work" was published in *Labour/Le Travail* 35 (Spring 1995). The essay is based on a presentation to the Island Institute's June 1994 Sitka Symposium, "The Spirit of Human Work," Sitka, AK.

The interview "To See the Truth of What Is / Is to Want to Change It" was published in a longer version entitled "An Interview With Tom Wayman" in *Contemporary Verse 2* 30.4 (Spring 2008).

"Why Profess What is Abhorred: The Rescue of Poetry" was published in a slightly shorter version in *Canadian Literature* 155 (Winter 1997).

The interview "Writing From the Edges" was published in a version entitled "Tom Wayman, A Poet Reconsidered: A Conversation" in *The Writer's Chronicle* 41.4 (February 2009).

"Banish" by Margaret Christakos, as excerpted from *Multitudes* (Coach House, 2013). Reprinted by permission of Coach House Books.

"Brainwashed" by David Clayton-Thomas. Copyright © 1968 (Renewed 1996), EMI Blackwood Music Inc. All right controlled and administered by EMI Blackwood Music Inc. All rights reserved. Used by permission.

"The Mary Ellen Carter" by Stan Rogers. Copyright © 1979 Stan Rogers/ Fogarty's Cove Music. All licensing administered by The Borealis Recording Company Ltd. Used by permission.

"San Antonio Girl": words and music by Lyle Lovett. Copyright © 2004 Universal-Polygram International Publishing, Inc. and Lylesongs. All Rights Controlled and Administered by Universal-Polygram International Publishing, Inc. All Rights Reserved. Used by Permission. *Reprinted by Permission of Hal Leonard LLC.*

"This is Simple": excerpt from *Late and Posthumous Poems*, copyright © 1988 by Fundacion Pablo Neruda, translation copyright © 1988 by Ben Belitt. Used by permission of Grove/Atlantic, Inc. Any third party use of this material, outside of this publication, is prohibited.

"Trudy and Dave": words and music by John Hiatt. Copyright © 1988 by Universal Music—Careers. International Copyright Secured. All Rights Reserved. *Reprinted by Permission of Hal Leonard LLC.*

"What About Me", written by Dino Valenti. Copyright © 1970 Dreaming Jewels Music (BMI). Dreaming Jewels Music (BMI) administered worldwide by Grow Your Own Music (BMI), a division of "A" Side Music d/b/a/ Modern Works Music Publishing. All Rights Reserved. Reprinted with Permission.

ABOUT THE AUTHOR

In 2015, a plaque on Vancouver's Commercial Drive commemorated Tom Wayman as a Vancouver Literary Landmark in recognition of his contribution to the city's literary heritage, specifically his championing of people writing for themselves about their daily employment. Wayman has explored the implications of this new work writing in two previous essay collections, *Inside Job* (1983) and *A Country Not Considered: Canada, Culture, Work* (1993). He has edited a number of anthologies of the new work poetry, most recently *Paperwork* (1991).

More than 20 collections of his own poems have been published since 1973, including *Dirty Snow* (2012) which won the Acorn-Plantos Award for People's Poetry. Two volumes of selected poems appeared in 2014, *The Order in Which We Do Things: The Poetry of Tom Wayman* (edited by Owen Percy) in Canada, and *Built to Take It: Selected Poems 1996-2013* in the U.S. His most recent poetry title is *Helpless Angels* (2017).

Two collections of Wayman's short fiction have been published, including *The Shadows We Mistake for Love* (2015), which won the inaugural 2016 Diamond Foundation Prize for Fiction. A book of his novellas, and a novel *Woodstock Rising* (2009) have also appeared.

Wayman has worked at a number of blue- and white-collar jobs across North America, and has been active in both mainstream and alternative unions as well as participating in a number of labor arts ventures. He was the founding president of the Kootenay School of the Arts Faculty and Staff Association bargaining unit.

For much of his working life, Wayman was a postsecondary teacher in both mainstream and alternative educational institutions. Most of his teaching career was spent in the B.C. community college system. He holds Associate Professor Emeritus of English status from the University of Calgary, where he taught 2002-2010. In 2007, he was the Fulbright Visiting Chair in Creative Writing at Arizona State University.

Wayman is a co-founder of the Vancouver Industrial Writers' Union, the Vancouver centre of the Kootenay School of Writing, the writing program of the Kootenay School of the Arts, and the Kootenay Literary Society. He has served as writer-in-residence at the universities of Windsor, Alberta, Simon Fraser, Winnipeg and Toronto.

Since 1989 he has been based in the Slocan Valley in southeastern B.C., where he is active in a number of community literary ventures.

Printed in February 2018
by Gauvin Press,
Gatineau, Québec